MAKING MICROPLANS

a community-based process in design and development

MAKING MICROPLANS

a community-based process in design and development

REINHARD GOETHERT and NABEEL HAMDI
with Sebastian Gray and Andrew Slettebak
Foreword by Otto Koenigsberger

IT PUBLICATIONS 1988

Intermediate Technology Publications Ltd
103/105 Southampton Row, London WC1B 4HH, UK

Acknowledgement

We would like to thank UNICEF Sri Lanka and the National Housing Development Authoritiy of Sri Lanka for providing major support and assistance for the research and development phases of this book.

ISBN 1 85339 085 2

Printed in Great Britain by The Short Run Press, Exeter

Abbreviations

NHDA:	National Housing Development Authority (Sri Lanka)
MIT:	Massachusetts Institute of Technology
JTO:	Junior Technical Officer
UNICEF:	United Nations Childrens Fund
PO:	Project Officer
HW:	Health warden
CDC:	Community Development Council
CMC:	Colombo Municipal Council

FOREWORD

This is a practical guide for community groups and their leaders; it is needed and will prove useful.

It is an account — or rather accounts — of several heterogeneous groups of people, some in Sri Lanka and some in Chile, who decided to get going and establish their own urban settlements. This did not necessarily mean 'with their own hands,' although manual labour was not excluded — in fact there was quite a lot of it, but the essential feature was that the future settlers and house owners were in charge; they hired help, procured materials and components and called for assistance from officials when they needed it.

This has lately become the preferred method of solving housing problems in the poorest of the many poor Third World countries which are rich in nothing but human labour, human ingenuity and genuine goodwill. It is also the only method that produces satisfaction among those for whom the settlements are intended. For those fortunate ones, it produces happy neighbourhoods.

Many learned and not-so-learned papers have been written on the subject of self-help settlements. Most of them tell us what an excellent solution self-help is in all its many forms, but few tell us what is the first step to translate a poor man's day-dreams into reality. How do you assemble and organize a group of volunteers for the tough and tiring job of house building: who leads and who follows, what help can you expect from the authorities, which is the right plot size for the purpose, how much land should you reserve for future growth, what do you do about recycling of waste materials, etc.? The MIT booklet about 'Microplanning' is not a reference work but, if read carefully, it will supply answers by telling us in detail what has happened in the three or four cases which it describes in great detail. The outcome is an excellent book that is both instructive and a pleasure to read.

Otto Koenigsberger
London

INTRODUCTION

Microplanning is a community-based process in design and development which enables programmes for neighbourhood upgrading to be prepared and implemented locally, collaboratively and quickly. It is a process for 'going to scale' based on building the capability locally to manage and act upon decisions, as well as to implement project work.

Its methods are neither proscriptive nor prescriptive of either content or procedure, and leave much room for improvisation. Instead, they provide structure for making decisions and relating decision-makers; a process which can be accessed at any one of its stages, whether it be identifying problems, setting priorities, working out general strategies or preparing for implementation. The starting point, in other words, is largely dependent on local circumstances and objectives.

Implicit, however, is an approach which is largely problem-driven and where each action in turn identifies subsequent actions, building the programme as one proceeds, rather than as pre-emptive or pre-packaged.

In this way, local participants can contribute not only to the content, but also to the structure of the programme. Only the broadest of intentions (or policies) are brought to the site from the top, and subsequently crafted into workable programmes from the bottom. Microplanning is a process which seeks to build linkages between local and central needs (or between local programmes and national policies) and so to reach consensus among participants on priorities, as well as appropriate courses of action and government intervention.

We now know that urban low-income settlements are usually both resourceful and problematic. However, while we do have substantial knowledge about the dynamics of these settlements, we do not as yet have a sound theory about practice. Therefore, in Microplanning, four assumptions are made on which the methods are built:

1. Problems of implementation arise not so much because people locally lack information or skills, but because they lack an adequate framework for articulating and prioritizing problems, defining solutions, and building consensus and partnerships.

2. Not enough mediation takes place between public and private organizations, and between funders and implementors and policies and projects.

3. There are not enough incentives for local production, with preference still for centralized and standard solutions as a basis for mass production.

4. Not enough learning takes place, and even when it does, it usually takes too long to find its way back into the mainstream of practice and usually winds up in thick reports that no one knows quite how to use.

A further assumption is the underlying issue in project upgrading of 'going to scale' and three key principles are suggested for achieving this: (1) more variety; (2) more participation; and (3) more learning.

This book is directed at those responsible for the management and implementation of small-scale community-based upgrading programmes. It is a tool with which to craft these programmes as well as to train local trainers in programming and design of such programmes.

Interactive community processes have been used in many fields before, and we have no pretensions that what is presented is fundamentally new or unique. Community participation has long been theorized, but few examples of strong successes exist. Our work has focused on bringing theory to practice, and the associated methods which make it work at the community scale. We have noted little documentation which makes explicit these techniques, and we have compiled this book with this goal in mind: to bring examples and suggestions for community-based programmes.

This book is a humble attempt to share the methods and experience of those who have practised Microplanning with others involved in the complex business of settlement upgrading. We have prepared this material specifically to elicit response and discussion. Rather than to instruct, we see this as a part of a continuing effort to communicate with colleagues. The question is *not* whether these methods are good or bad, or different, or any better than anyone else's. More useful, do they contain ideas which can be carried forward and built upon?

In this respect, a number of questions remain unanswered. Are the results any more effective from any other project? Or, if not, do the means employed offer greater equity or efficiency, or are they any more cost-effective? Has the money and effort been better directed with Microplanning than without it? Does the consensus-building process, which we do by first inducing a convergence of interests and later a convergence of interpretation about where the real problems or opportunities lie, better direct our interventions? Do they unlock ideas and solutions which may otherwise remain hidden? Does the spirit of co-operation established between professionals, government, community, and health workers, add up to anything substantive when it comes to doing the job? Are people better off with Microplanning than without it, or is this a process which largely benefits urban managers? We have only begun to inform some of these questions.

The methods have been developed over the last two years or so, and tested in various countries and under varying socio-political and physical conditions.

Section I deals with the theory and practice of Microplanning. In the first chapter the theoretical basis to the approach is mapped, and its assumptions and objectives in the context of current trends are clarified. In Chapter Two, the methods are illustrated in practice, through a community-based workshop undertaken in La Pintana, a low-income community outside of Santiago, Chile. In the third chapter, we track the implementation of one sample programme developed in Sri Lanka, where the results of community-based workshops were carried through to implementation. In Section II, the handbook is included in full for readers to carry out their own workshops.

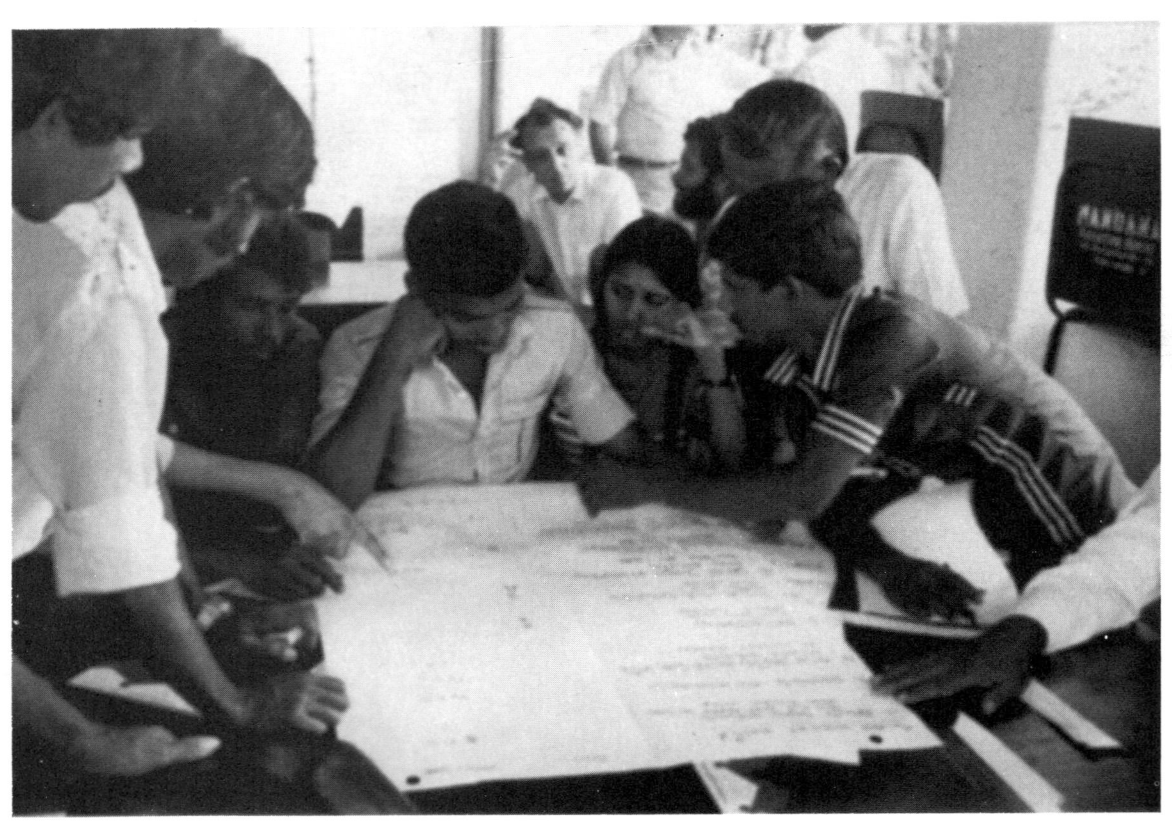

ACKNOWLEDGEMENTS

The work contained in this book has been greatly assisted by numerous individuals and organizations, to whom we are indebted. Its basic theories were initially developed during our research in Egypt, which was sponsored by the Technology Adaptation Programme of MIT and assisted by the General Organization of Physical Planning (GOPP), in Cairo. The developmental phases culminating in the handbook presented in Section III were sponsored by UNICEF, Sri Lanka, and by the National Housing Development Authority (NHDA) of Sri Lanka, both of whom were instrumental in evaluating the methods, providing valuable insights into its practical implications, and organizing the local workshops. Particular thanks go to the Government of Sri Lanka, whose innovative Million Houses Programme provided the needed supportive setting for research and experimentation.

Thanks also go to the Department of Architecture at MIT, who through their Grunsfeld Research Incentive Fund enabled further development and testing of the work in Santiago, Chile. The Escuela de Arquitectura, Universidad Católica de Chilé, deserves special mention for their critical and resourceful collaboration with us, for undertaking important preliminary work and for producing a companion report which was a valuable resource for this volume. Also to officials of the Municipality of La Pintana, all of whom made the workshop in La Pintana a profound learning experience.

Special thanks to all the students at MIT and the University Catolica, to the professional staff of the NHDA and UNICEF, and to residents of the various settlements in Sri Lanka and Chile in which we worked, for providing critical evaluations and contributing to and overseeing our research and for all the leg work involved in making the arrangements.

SECTION 1

1. SETTING THE CONTEXT
2. RUNNING A WORKSHOP
3. LEARNING FROM IMPLEMENTATION

1.
SETTING THE CONTEXT

INTRODUCTION

We know that urban settlement upgrading is a complex business. It is characterized by innumerable groups of people with competing vested interests, conflicting values and priorities, and by fragile yet productive networks and relationships, high densities, petty economies and technically difficult-to-service neighbourhoods. Statistical information is hard to get, and even when it is not, it often hides as much as it reveals. Governments want quick visible results which can rapidly expand the scale of their operation, but find themselves encumbered with processes and conditions which do not fit their general schema nor any general theory of planning and with which they are ill equipped to deal. What they confront are processes which are spontaneous, intuitive, incremental, mostly unregulated and with a large measure of adhocism.

And what they confront are people who *like* 'planning' because it gives them more than they had before, but *mistrust* it because they always get less than they expect.

In developing the Microplanning methods, and with these general issues in mind, we have borrowed principally from the effective and everyday ways in which most informal settlements emerge and consolidate, most housing gets built and most problems actually do get solved, one way or another.

Entrepreneurs emerge who service these settlements as moneylenders, materials manufacturers and suppliers, water vendors, garbage collectors and builders. Intricate and complex social, economic and political networks develop for purchasing and exchanging commodities, exerting influence, buying into services, securing employment and sometimes levering a stake in the general body politic of the urban or regional districts in which they are placed.

In time, people build a substantial body of experience about how best to build, to profit, or dodge the authorities. It is a cyclical process of doing and learning built up through individual experiences but institutionalized as knowledge, which is then passed on to others in a variety of formal and informal ways and which grows exponentially. If things go wrong, or do not work as well as expected, no one need step in with elaborate explanations. People will usually know what they do or do not need and usually have a theory about why something does or does not work.

If it was a land invasion which got things started, someone will have prepared 'starter plans,' setting out a few simple rules for who will get what and where, reserving lines of access and circulation, and establishing lines of least resistance for invasion and building. If it was not land invasion, these rules may have been set through, for example, the sale of agricultural subdivisions which will regulate the pace and form of development.

Within this general framework — which itself will consolidate and become 'specific' as time goes on — people will invent rules as they go, tailor-made to needs, aspirations, income and profit. The market place, both formal and informal, will have much to say about what happens, as will respected elders and traditions.

These processes we now consider both resourceful and in many ways problematic. Resourceful because they are fast, ingenious, full of inventive surprises and highly productive. Partnerships and organizations emerge if and when they are needed and, as important, disappear when they are not. In contrast to conventional wisdom, at least until recently, these settlements are evidence of cities which are healthy and working. Problematic because cities develop unpredictably (the best cities always did) and are therefore strained in terms of services, utilities and government, and because these same settlements suffer acute poverty, disease and political unrest.

Whatever the case, these settlements are dynamic, hopelessly unrigorous in conventional planning terms, and unstoppable. They are settlements with which governments are learning to live, having failed to stop them. The issues at stake are not new to development theorists nor to housing practitioners. The question still, however, is how to turn this current body of knowledge into sound practice. And in turn, how to practise at a scale commensurate with demand.

This book describes one method which tackles these two questions in the context of the conditions described above. It is a support-planning approach to urban upgrading based on theories of prescriptive action rather than prescriptive planning or design. It is an approach to planning and design concerned less with telling people what to do, than with describing how to find out what to do, and then how to generate alternatives for doing it. Its basic principles were first derived from our research with the Central Office of Physical Planning in Egypt, and subsequently developed and tested several times in Sri Lanka and Chile. They are directed at local administrative and technical staff from various levels of government for managing the processes of programme preparation, implementation and monitoring.

We have called the operational side of these efforts 'Making Microplans', because they are result-oriented, locally enacted, and deal in the first place with sites rather than urban districts or national strategies.

ASSUMPTIONS

The approach is based on a number of assumptions, raising issues which have been troublesome so far in practice, and need more study.

First, neither lack of *knowledge* about place nor *ability* to tackle problems are at issue in the business of upgrading. Technical skills are usually available albeit in rudimentary form, but sufficient to deal with the problems at hand. At the community level awareness of what works and what does not is rarely an issue, as the problems are known and finite. What is lacking in most cases is a forum for articulation of a problem, a framework that provides the structure for drawing out problems, defining solutions, and building consensus and partnerships.

Second, not enough mediation takes place between the demands of public authorities, and those of private or individual communities. There is a lack of consensus among those involved about problems, issues, objectives, priorities and actions.

What we need is a way of crafting workable links between various sets of demands, various groups of people, and various scales of organization which so often compete for dominance and so exclude the benefits which each has to bring to the design and planning processes.

We need to mediate between the need for some measure of strategic planning, setting longer term objectives with their implicit requirement to create reforms to improve conditions generally, and an equal demand for spontaneous, more intuitive action to enable problems to be solved immediately, locally, profitably, and as they arise. We need a way of disentangling public agencies from private organizations, and strategic planning (large, usually public organizations, national objectives, strategic plans) from problem solving (small, usually private organizations, local objectives, action plans). We need a process which is bottom up in terms of problem solving and top down in terms of co-ordination and management. But we need both with some measure of balance, and each with a large measure of give and take.

Too much co-ordination or strategic planning will slow things down. It will inhibit the ability to act spontaneously, finding this usually threatening to its order, and therefore to its objectives. It will tip the balance in favour of general needs or policy and will be too abstract to the people for whom it is intended, who will have to accept their objectives without really knowing why.

Too much spontaneity, on the other hand, is threatening and abstract for the government. In this situation, the government will be unable to control the pace of development, the allocation of land, standards of construction, the supply of money, materials, or infrastructure.

Where the demands of these two positions when taken together remain unresolved, as they so often do, governments usually adopt a position of appeasement. Projects are built which may be visible, but which are simplistic responses to complex issues and are thus short term in benefit. Most governments (and their supporting agencies) after all are committed to spending their budget in the time allocated and to meeting political pledges which gained them power. And so they will respond, for example, to the need for health improvement by building hospitals which we later find are inaccessible to those most in need, to housing by building houses which we later find the poor cannot afford, to play by building playgrounds which we later find no one uses; and so on. These projects serve little purpose, locally or generally, other than political expediency. The problems, at best, do not go away.

The third assumption is that not enough people are encouraged locally in production. Systems of production cease to be self-regulating and become self-serving.

This issue has been well illustrated in the analysis of large technology systems and four conclusions are reached: such systems encourage (1) centralization of control, (2) development of a technical elite, (3) decision-making processes that consider the needs of the system rather than the needs of outsiders affected by the system (i.e. the public), and (4) the development of mechanisms to prevent external criticism or to discredit those who may make it.

Fourth, despite the importance placed on project monitoring and evaluation, not enough learning takes place. And even if it does, it usually winds up documented in extensive reports which no knows quite how to use. While these reports represent a substantial accumulation of data and sometimes analysis, they remain non-operational. If they were, we might avoid repeating the same mistakes in design and planning, in project after project. There are of course all kinds of people who make evaluations, numerous reasons why they do so, and various methods which are used. There will have been municipal authorities, political groups, international funding agencies, central government housing authorities, church groups, user groups, architects, planners and engineers, all of whom will have had some say — some more than others — in programming and implementation. Most likely, each will have been looking to judge outcomes based on its own history of success or failure, to validate its approach, invalidate its competitors' approches, safeguard the status quo or get more work. Each party will be selective about what it measures and how it measures what it sees. Unfortunately, most monitoring ends up as little more than book-keeping and most evaluations are self-serving. Neither has much to do with learning.

METHOD AND PROCEDURE

We have considered three inseparable functions which form the basis of support planning: *the management of decision-making, design and training.*

The approach argues the first, largely in mediating between the demands of various vested-interest groups, building consensus, facilitating partnerships and generating options for project planning and implementation. For design is a process of enablement in designating minimal physical and regulatory frameworks which support lots of solution types, and which can be discovered progressively over a much longer time than conventional projects. It is a process which is of necessity (rather than good will) intensely participatory. Within the approach, training and therefore learning functions as a dynamic process, because we want to avoid building a 'static body of knowledge,' unlinked as we go to practice, and because we want to build a cadre of officials capable in their role as support planners. We need, in other words, a way of learning which enables knowledge to find its way back into the mainstream of practice, quickly and progressively.

The following pages will illustrate the first only of these functions, focusing largely on the Microplanning tool with which to practise the approach.

Microplanning is directed at addressing three general and familiar questions: What is wrong? What could be done to put things right? How to go about doing it?

The approach therefore includes procedures which are grouped under five related areas of action and analysis:

1. Problem identification

2. General strategies to deal with problems

3. Programme agreement, assessing actions, options and trade-offs

4. Implementation planning

5. Monitoring and evaluation

The first of these has to do with the way we see and therefore with coming to grips with the physical and social make-up of place. It involves documentation and analysis — what have we got and how do things work? What are the problems, why and for whom, and in what order of priority? What implicit opportunities are available?

The second is about strategy: What alternative general approaches might we adopt, given available resources, to solve or manage problems, and to build on or profit from opportunities? It follows that for each general approach there will be alternative routes to take to turn general strategies into specific action.

The third category of question then is: what are these actions and how do they reflect priorities? And for each, what are the trade-offs in terms of money, administration, or technical feasibility, amongst others?

The fourth category concerns itself largely with how best to get the job done. It involves the kinds of questions which articulate a plan of action for implementation: how do we start things off, what are the tasks, who does what, when and how?

Lastly, as work gets under way, there will be a double agenda for those involved with implementation, particularly the technical and management teams.

First, and inevitably, as priorities change, as technical and administrative problems reveal themselves, as the supply of money, materials and even political goodwill dry up, we will want to know what lessons or principles we can derive from what we are doing or have done, to finish the job at hand effectively. Secondly, we might want to ask: what can we learn this time to improve performance next time? What would one do differently next time assuming one confronted similar sets of circumstances? And in this sense, what general indices or guidelines might we discover which would be helpful next time for project work? This process of learning or reflecting in action we commonly call monitoring and evaluation, although as we have argued, it less commonly serves that purpose. It is the fifth and often sadly lacking category of inquiry. We adopt the following sample procedure during the programming phase, usually conducted in about three days and as a workshop on site.

1. Problem identification

- In Step 1, procedures are delineated for making short, sample surveys with checklists of 'What to look for'.
- In Step 2, the various problems as identified and perceived by each group are defined, with an indication of why and for whom these problems exist.
- In Step 3, game playing techniques are used as a tool with which to agree on problems, and their level of priority. The outcome is a list of those problem areas which all agree are critical, and an equivalent list which one or another party feels to be important, but cannot get agreement on.

2. General strategies

The goal is to identify alternative ways in which the critical problems identified above can be tackled, and to have these prioritized. Again, three steps are outlined with specific procedures and checklists of things to consider whilst proceeding.

- In Step 1, each interest group prioritizes the strategies which it thinks may be appropriate, with some indication of those that are immediate, or urgent and need to be tackled now, and those that can wait until later.

- In Step 2, through negotiation, the group agrees on a summary list of actions.
- In Step 3, these are prioritized by all parties.

3. Agreeing on a programme

The goal here is to identify several appropriate ways of carrying out the strategies treated above, and then to select the most appropriate, based on the balance between feasibility and desirability. Two essential steps for doing this are considered.

- In Step 1, a list is made of the alternative ways in which a strategy can be carried out, and an overall cost index is attached, based on the assumption that the work will be done entirely through formal government contract channels. The project team (which includes the ultimate beneficiaries) is then able to offset this cost by negotiating and agreeing alternative levels of community involvement in doing the work.
- In Step 2, the project team is asked to decide which options are most technically feasible, affordable, and desirable. As more information becomes available, and as discussions continue, it may be necessary to revert to Step 1 and to renegotiate the community input.

4. Planning for implementation

In this section, the objective is to establish a step-by-step procedure for the implementation of the programme as agreed above. The outcome — a set of action plans — delineates the who, what and how, relative to the work to be done and defines in more detail the physical planning requirements for dealing with improvements and additions to both site and dwellings. In this case, four steps for doing this are delineated, with checklists and other supportive procedural material.

- During the first step, each part of the programme to be implemented is scheduled, together with the tasks involved, and who does them and how.
- In Step 2, site improvements are planned including the new addition as located in the plan, and checked against local conditions, and in Step 3 a similar procedure is adopted for the house.
- In Step 4, a detailed schedule of how to proceed is drawn up, together with where to start and when, for all the agreed components of the project. Thus the action plan is inclusive of proposals which also link physical improvements with other social and health programmes (community development plan, health education, technical skills development training, etc.).

No process, however, is in practice linear. It does not matter in reality where one starts, or which way one moves. It does matter that each step has a basis in theory as well as in practice and that we therefore link what we think should be done with what we know is most likely to work.

And so, in searching for answers, there will be theories with which to describe why things work the way they do, general concepts to deal with them, and methods for interpreting these strategies into workable plans. If these theories, concepts, and methods do not exist, they will have to be invented.

In addition, and most importantly, there will be the real world to which all three will need to conect. Unless they do, they will have little value and even less chance of success. Understanding, in this respect, will need to be grounded on observation of the facts as they exist, and as they are described by those whose daily lives they affect. We will gain only a partial understanding of these facts if we base our search on systems of analysis which usually direct research and planning towards questions which can be quantified and modeled, and away from those that cannot. Moreover, general concepts or strategies have to be turned into actions which are workable locally, and methods of implementation will need to be turned into contracts, partnerships and money which fit with local resources, local administrative capabilities and political realities.

We need to ground good practice in sound theory and vice versa, if we are to avoid, on the one hand, the kind of utopian visions which have so far been troublesome in practice; and on the other, the kind of perfunctory practice which contributes little to the general body of principles on which we base theory and with which we craft policy. Put another way, the field in this respect remains divided. In one camp, there are the empiricists with their view that experience is the only source of knowledge, and in the other the rationalists arguing that reason alone, rather than authority or intuition provides a valid basis for knowledge. In many ways we agree with both positions, and therefore with neither camp.

An example will illustrate. In one case, the need identified was that of a health clinic. After preliminary analysis, local officials argued that a clinic existed within a short bus ride for most families, and that investment in building this type of facility was neither justified nor necessary. In theory they were right, in practice they were wrong. Right, yes, because their investment in building could not be justified given their reasoning and the money it would entail. Wrong because the problem had been wrongly defined. Further analysis revealed the real issue was not the *availability* of a clinic, but *accessibility* to it. People were intimidated by the formal procedures for making appointments (which, in the absence of telephones, usually required at least two trips), by the long wait once there (for which they might lose a day's income), by the preference given to those of higher income or class, and by the expense of the bus ride itself.

In theory, therefore, little or no intervention would have been contemplated. Even if it had, in line with the initial request, it would have been wrongly directed. In practice, however, it was recognized that a problem did exist, and that it was both real and immediate. Some general approaches for putting things right were prepared. These included a mobile service facility, converting an existing disused building into a medical centre, and creating a special unit within the existing clinic to expedite diagnosis and treatment. In practice, however, the medical team argued that the most common cause of complaint was diarrhoea, and its associated symptom of dehydration. If this was so, they argued, then local paramedics might be trained to identify symptoms and to train families in the use of oral rehydration, a simple self-administered procedure which would relieve the burden on local medical administrations, speed the process up, and save life. When symptoms were not diagnosed locally, families would continue to be referred to the existing clinic, where, however, paramedics would mediate between families and doctors.

What emerged therefore, was a number of actions which would fit local circumstances. They included training, a well-tried process of self-help treatment, and locally staffed informal clinics serviced periodically by a mobile unit. What might have been a simple single response to a given problem became a package of responses, a *system* more suited to the scale of demand and the complexities of conditions actually encountered. This was made possible by linking cyclically perceived problems (observation) with actual problems (analysis), general approaches and specific actions.

The preceding example, together with the assumptions we have outlined, highlight a number of principles which now form the basis of the Microplanning approach.

First, if we are to keep pace with the unprecedented demand for shelter services and utilities, (which we have not done so far) and avoid reducing complex processes to simplistic formulae, then we will need to work at the kind of scale which few single organizations, however large, have so far been able to do. Second, if we are to tackle the issue of scale effectively, we will need to rethink our approaches in respect of three additional correlative demands: more variety (production, building, delivery), more participation and more learning. Unlike conventional philosophy, large-scale production is not only compatible with these three correlatives, but necessarily dependent on them. The more ways you can go for acquiring land, materials, money, employment, shelter and services and the more people and organizations involved, the more likely you are to move quickly, and in ways more fitting to the needs and limits of available resources. Moving quickly, however, we now know means moving incrementally (slowly?). In Microplanning, therefore, the task is to identify where best to *start* (with the emphasis on process), rather than how best to *finish* (with the emphasis on product). Once decided, there will be the task of aggregating each link during the various phases of improvement, building more powerful systems or principles of procedure for the *delivery of better housing*, utilities and services, rather than *production of better houses*, schools or hospitals.

It follows that few of these processes can be enacted to the exclusion of the people for whom they are intended. The principle of participatory planning and design is therefore important here in two ways. It is important technically as a way of making design, production, management and maintenance more efficient. It is important socially, because without a large measure of self-determination, ownership and control, people will usually wait around, if something needs doing, for someone to come along and do it. And when, as is most often the case, that someone does not come along, apathy and resentment set in, and environments deteriorate rapidly in physical, political and social terms.

Participation means partnership, connecting horizontally amongst people of equal status (not necessarily equal power), and vertically between those who set policies and those who live within the framework of those policies. And partnership means not only that one shares *in* the action of others, but is involved *with* others, developing options, negotiating priorities and agreeing on directions. Unless one is involved, the process will be perfunctory, as illustrated by Arnstein. She pointed out that in the United States, ‘Survey after survey has documented that poor housewives most want tot-lots in their neighbourhood where young children can play safely. But most women answered the questionnaire without knowing what their options were. They assumed that if they asked for something small, they might just get something useful in their neighbourhoods. Had the mothers known that a free pre-paid health insurance plan was a possible option, they might not have put tot-lots so high on their lists.'

Both scale and speed require the accumulation of knowledge which helps improve performance as we go along. Learning and therefore training become an integral part of the Microplanning approach in ways which are dynamic, based on discovery rather than curricula.

Three principles are critical here: the first is time, the second is relevance and the third is partnership. Time, because we cannot afford to lock ourselves into months or sometimes years of costly evaluation; relevance because we want to judge what is transferable from site to site, place to place and even culture to culture; and partnership because not only do we seek to understand our action through the eyes of other parties with whom we have been involved, but also because we want to understand how and why they see what they see in the way they do.

PRINCIPLES STRATEGIES AND TACTICS

The Microplanning approach is not what one would normally associate with upgrading strategies: (1) it is not an 'advocacy' approach; (2) it is not essentially a participation approach, but a joint decision-sharing approach where all parties have equal standing; and (3) it does not require time or continuing support to function.

The Microplanning approach is developed around the following considerations:

The process is problem driven

The identification and articulation of problems provides the basis for the pro cess. Although entry may occur at any of the stages, the driving considerations are problems, and the formulation of alternative solutions.

The definition of what consistutes a problem is open-ended: what people *think* are problems, as well as what most others would agree are 'real' problems are treated equally.

In learning from previous projects, the converse of 'problems', i.e., opportunities, is added, to stress what also went well.

The process is essentially a strong framework

The process prescribes a set of steps with a clearly articulated procedure to be followed by the various actors. Even so, only the *objectives* of each stage are important. The sequence and steps in each stage are variable, and can be adjusted to fit the circumstances. The 'precision' of the framework is indeed its quality of uncertainty about results, and so its order is in its operation rather than in its goals. Encouragement is given to experimentation and to tailoring the process to the personality of the workshop leaders and the structure of the agencies.

The process is interactive and interdisciplinary

A vital element is the interaction and exchange between the various actors: community representatives, technical staff from public agencies, and political representatives. A variety of staff may be involved: health workers, social workers, architects, engineers, etc.

The process considers variable time-frames

The focus of effort is clearly short-term and immediate, defined as things which can be done within a year, more or less. However, long-term concerns are also extracted and made explicit. These are defined in several ways: (1) those requiring a higher order of planning; (2) those requiring a particular technical skill; (3) those that need to be co-ordinated with several other agencies; and (4) those that require substantial or new budget allocations.

The process is cyclical and allows ready feedback

The medium of interaction is charts that are filled in by the various groups during each stage of the workshop. This stress on explicit *documentation* is premised by two notions: (1) the process of writing descriptions sharpens the thinking of the participants and draws out commitments, and (2) the charts allow *traceability* or review and awareness of the steps taken in reaching a conclusion. This allows clear backtracking and modification of a decision if later considerations identify new conditions.

Information (data) remains internalized, and is not extracted

Instead of the time-consuming and costly extraction of the data in the community, the data sources (the users) directly participate. Data is only needed as a reference to identify key problems, and is not necessary for its own sake. An added advantage is that data comes with values, and does not remain as raw, unprioritized information.

The process encourages and promotes community leadership

Development of local leaders is promoted through the participation format in the workshops. Reinforcement of the local community structure occurs by the community's active participation in decisions. Formal recognition of a spokesman for each group by both the authorities and the other members of the community reinforces the existing leadership. In cases where no leadership exists, the workshop provides an opportunity to identify and test potential leaders.

Because of the groups and the interactive format, each individual is encouraged to contribute, and each individual view is valued.

The process is locally based and biased toward community interests.

The issues and priorities of the community are the focus. Their demands, however, may be modified later by policy and larger strategic considerations.

To reinforce the community bias, the workshop is held on-site in the community, either in the local school, community centre, religious building, or even in the open.

Advantages of basing the workshop locally are: (1) it reinforces the bias towards the community; and (2) it allows involvement by other community members normally excluded, i.e., women and children (Yes, children! A workshop in Sri Lanka dealt with play areas — passing children became respondents to the proposals and provided instant feedback.).

The process promotes self-reliance

The workshop encourages the community to evaluate its capacity to effect changes on its own, without direct government assistance. The format encourages and makes explicit the notion that communities can satisfy many needs through local resources, and thus 'stretch' limited government capabilities into those areas it cannot do on its own.

The process is built on the successive filtering of issues and priorities

The process goes from an open-ended list of problems to a few specific, carefully thought-out priority concerns of the community. The initial list contains all the issues that participants are able to identify, with the assumption that things that bother people will be most prominent when recalling concerns. Each stage filters and sharpens the concerns, with the technique and criteria changing in each stage. The filtering process enables one to constantly check disputable facts and issues as one proceeds. This is achieved in several ways:

(1) Time — only a short period is allowed to reach a decision and make a listing.
(2) Space — the charts only allow a summary of key points, and only a limited number of points can be dealt with. (Although extra charts are available in order not to omit any pressing concerns, this involves additional effort, and is a braking factor.)
(3) Process — each stage demands choice between a limited number of alternatives, primarily in two ways: (a) by reaching a consensus within the group, and (b) by reaching a consensus with other groups. This eliminates less supportable or less strongly argued concerns.

The process has a built-in follow-up bias

Chances of implementing the agreed work programme are more assured by several built-in tactics. The community is assigned the primary pressure role, because it has the strongest interest in success.
(1) The authorities and the community generally both contribute their efforts, i.e., both provide input and thus each may pressurize the other to follow through. (On the other hand, each may blame the other for failure to deliver, and thus not contribute.)
(2) An agreement is publicly signed by representatives from both the community and the authorities, with the entire community invited to act as observers. The entire community thus provides additional pressure on implementation of the agreements.
(3) A specific date for reporting to the community is set publicly, making failure to deliver more problematic.
(4) The signed agreement remains on display in a public area of the community, constantly reminding everyone of the agreements.

The process balances power interests

Difficulties can arise when community members are reluctant to express their concerns. Reasons tend to fall into two catagories: the fear of authority, and the arrogance of the technical staff. These fears are mitigated by several inherent workshop techniques:
(1) Community representatives are selected to overwhelm numerically the authorities and the technical staff. The greater the fear of authority, the more community members should be involved.
(2) Spokesmen are always selected from community respresentatives, and others are prohibited from presenting, specifically excluding the technical staff and government representatives.

What is needed for the approach to be institutionalized into an agency structure?

No substantive modification is required, nor are fundamental revisions needed in the structure of an agency. However, three aspects are basic, and are generally already inherent in most agencies dealing with housing programmes.
(1) A clearly recognized contact person must be available throughout the process, and the subsequent follow-up. A project officer or equivalent is the ideal person. The contact is not limited to the role of an intermediary, but ideally has a technical/implementation responsibility as well.
(2) Funds allocated to an area targeted for upgrading must allow for flexibility in their allocation. This suggests that a 'lump sum' approach for budgeting is necessary. (The issue then, of course, becomes one of how much the lump sum should be, etc.) Less ideally, a wide range of programmes could be drawn on to support varied needs of the community, as arise out of the work programme in the workshop.
(3) A mechanism for carrying out Microplans must be established. Because of the simplicity and short duration, this is generally not a limiting factor.

How can a Microplanning workshop team be established?

Several approaches may be used in setting up a programme. The specific situation of each country would determine which would be most appropriate.

- Establishment of a separate training cadre. This group would become a special section in an agency, and would carry out development workshops as needed. The advantage is that the cadre has direct contact with current policy decisions.
- Combining an outside workshop leader, perhaps from an area university, with a training team from an agency. The workshop leader would be selected for demonstrated teaching skills. This outsider would provide a neutral perspective to consensus building and would be less likely to be identified with one group or another. School teachers may be likely candidates because of their teaching experience.
- Selecting leaders from a community who have undergone a Microplanning workshop.

Initial workshops would be set up on an experimental basis with the intention of learning and refining procedures. Then, leaders selected from workshops would in turn carry out workshops in other areas. In this model the leaders would represent a neutral entity with experience in communities and empathy for situations not understood by or divergent with agency policy.

OPEN QUESTIONS

Several questions remain and will need further study. Answers may be found as the process is further tested in a variety of other contexts.

What if some of the actors will not 'play'?

Could the reluctance to concede control and decision-sharing in a community result in a breakdown of the participation by the authorities? Are sufficient incentives built in to assure active participation by all of the representatives?

How does one know if the problems are 'real'?

How is current fashion separated from fundamental problems? Should current, short-term concerns be excluded? Should up-front surveys still be carried out to provide a basis for information? Should after-the-fact surveys be carried out to verify conclusions?

What if the process moves too fast?

Since the approach is quick, it may easily overload the capacity to deliver. As one moves from site to site, will government agencies have the capacity to process the many plans in relatively short periods of time?

How are areas selected?

Since the approach offers a technique to service many areas quickly, should all communities undergo a Microplanning workshop? If not, how will areas be prioritized and targeted for improvement? Can the process be used to prioritize among neighbourhoods, as well as among specific problems within each neighbourhood?

How can it be assured that a community is 'fairly' represented?

LONG-TERM IMPLICATIONS

1. Housing is no longer a limitation, for the perspective is now shifted to a broader base of concerns, ranging from health, community development, education, employment, transportation, as well as the traditional housing and infrastructure concerns.

2. Use of Microplanning implies a change from a housing agency into a multifaceted government interface agency.

3. Microplanning pushes a government into power-sharing because of the joint decision-making process.

4. The role of consultants now changes. Once a structure is established, consultants may now revert to traditional forms of technical support as their only remaining role.

SELECTIVE READING

Action. *Project Evaluation Handbook (Vol. 1); Program Monitoring Handbook (Vol. 2); Assessing Performance: A Reference Series for the Field*. Action, Washington, D.C., 1981.

Argyris, C., Putnam, R., and McCain Smith, D. *Action Science — Concepts, Methods, and Skills for Research and Intervention*. Josey-Bass Publications, San Francisco, London, 1985.

Berger, P.L. and R.J. Neuhaus. *To Empower People — The Role of Mediating Structures in Public Policy*. American Enterprise Institute for Public Policy Research; Washington, D.C., August 1979.

Feuerstein, Marie-Therese. *Partners in Evaluation: Evaluating Development and Community Programmes with Participants*. Macmillan Publishers, New York, 1986.

Goethert, R. and N. Hamdi. 'Rapid Site Planning for Refugees — A Procedural Primer for Land, Shelter, Infrastructure and Services'. Unpublished, UNHCR, Geneva, 1987.

Lindblom, Charles, E. 'The Science of Muddling Through.' *Public Administration Review*, Vol. 19. p. 79. Spring, 1959.

Fisher, Roger, and William Ury, with Bruce Patton, Editor. *Getting to Yes: Negotiating Agreement Without Giving In*. Penguin Books, New York, 1981.

McGill, M.E. and M.E. Horton. *Action Research Designs — For Training and Development*. National Training and Development Press, Washington, D.C., 1973.

Paul, Samuel. *Community Participation*. World Bank Discussion Paper Number 6. The World Bank, Washington, D.C., 1987.

Peattie, Lisa. 'Realistic Planning and Qualitative Research', *Habitat International*, 7, 5/6; 1983.

Silverman, Jerry M., Merlyn Kettering, and Terry D. Schmidt. *Action — Planning Workshops for Development Management: Guidelines*. World Bank Technical Paper Number 56. The World Bank, Washington, D.C., 1986.

Silverman, Jerry M. *Technical Assistance and Aid Agency Staff: Alternative Techniques for Greater Effectiveness*. World Bank Technical Paper Number 28. The World Bank, Washington, D.C., 1984.

Stretton, Hugh. *Urban Planning in Rich and Poor Countries*. Oxford University Press, Oxford, 1978.

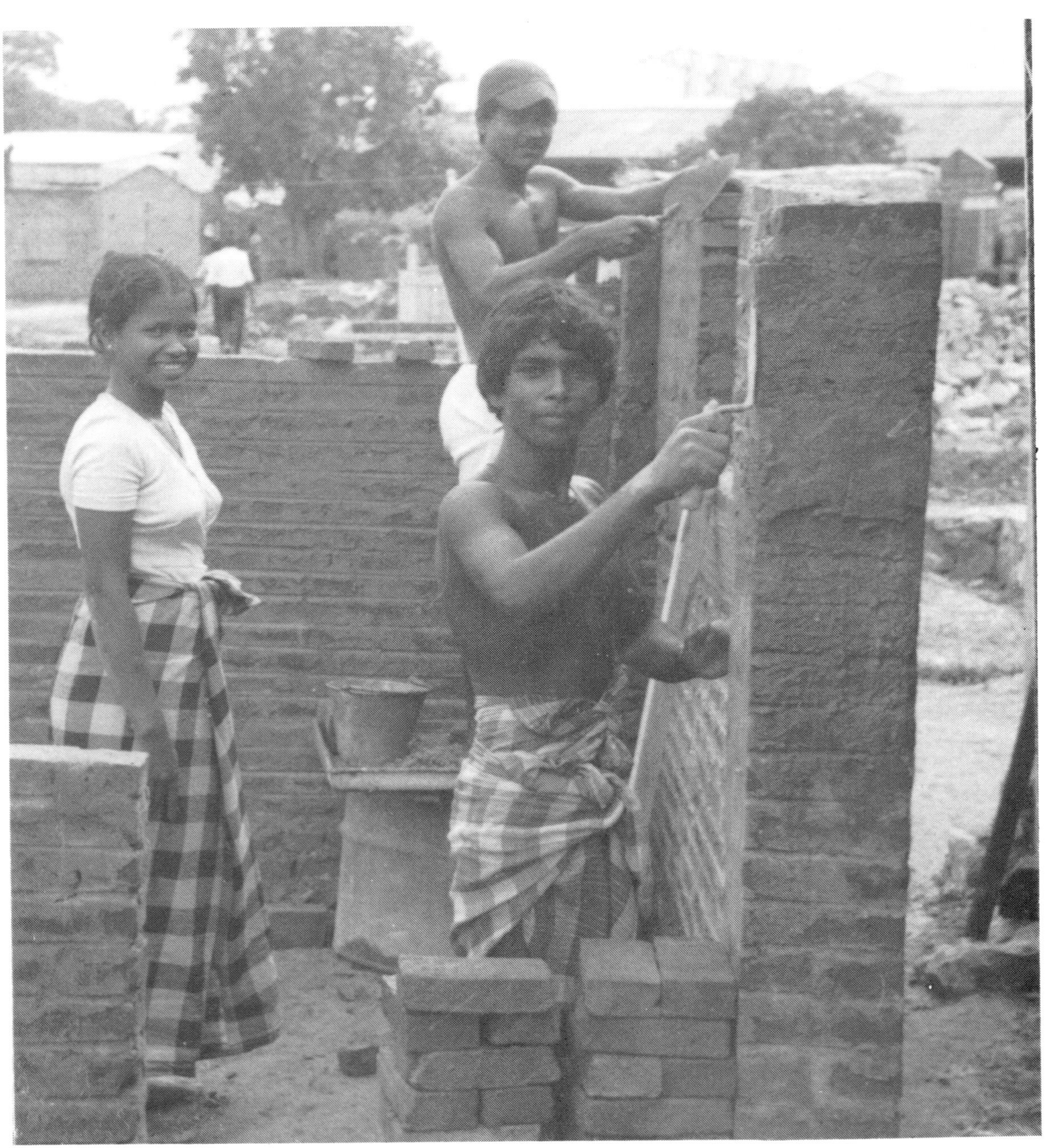

2. RUNNING A WORKSHOP

UPGRADING AT VILLA GABRIELA CHILE

DESCRIPTION OF THE WORKSHOP

The Microplanning approach was demonstrated in a workshop held at La Pintana, on the outskirts of Santiago, Chile. The intention of this workshop was to explore a joint university effort to use the diverse public housing settlements in Santiago as a laboratory for continued study. To this end, people from both schools, the Municipality of La Pintana, the Housing Ministry, the UN, local churches and the settlement at Villa Gabriela participated in the interactive workshop described on the following pages. This section relates the author's first-hand view, not as a participant, but as an observer familiar with housing study. The text, pictures and reproductions of the participants' work that follow present a brief documentation of the La Pintana workshop and the Microplanning approach as it was used in practice.

Introducing the workshop

The workshop begins with an explanation of two sets of objectives. The first set forms the immediate agenda:

(1) Local *problems and opportunities* are identified and ordered.
(2) Optional *strategies* to improve conditions are developed.
(3) Participants draw *general lessons* for other projects.

These three stages are based upon the broader, second set of objectives — those of the approach. The objectives of the approach are described as key concerns in all settlement planning:

- First objective is the *speed* of the approach; in the past, too much has been invested without physical results; so this approach minimizes study and maximizes action.

• Second is the *participation* of everyone involved, so that consensus can be used to make the identification of both problem and solution meaningful.

• The third objective is that of *scale*. It is important to those organizing the workshop, that the planning methods demonstrated are replicable. If others are trained, the effects can increase progressively.

The explanation of objectives raises a few questions. Two of the local participants voice a common concern: they want to do more than help students with their degrees.

Forming groups, and the first exercise

The participants count off to form three groups, each with about seven members. They are asked to select a spokesman. Four university members who were active in the organization of the workshop are divided between the groups. The workshop leader asks each to act as a facilitator — someone that can assist the group if needed.

Two large sheets of paper are given to each group. Following the workshop leader's instructions, the sheets are folded into three columns — a simple action bringing the participants into immediate contact. The results of the first exercise will be written on these sheets for presentation and discussion.

Everyone is asked to spend forty-five minutes walking in the settlement. Three considerations are to be noted:

(1) What are the problems and opportunities in the Settlement?

(2) Why is it a problem or an opportunity?

(3) For whom is it a consideration?

Before leaving for the field survey, the workshop leader suggests that some participants limit themselves to visual observation while others base their findings on conversation with settlement residents. In this way a range of problems and opportunities can be identified from different viewpoints and ways of seeing.

CAMPAMENTO NUEVO AMANECER

Y LA VILLA GABRIELA MISTRAL

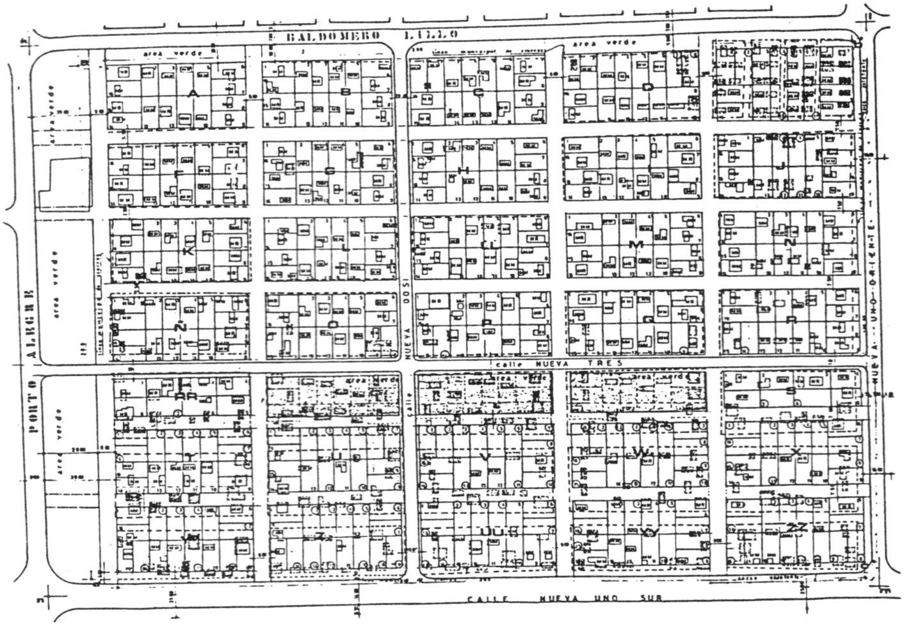

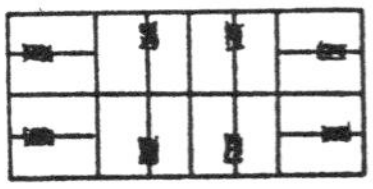

BALDOMERO LILLO

PORTO ALEGRE

calle NUEVA TRES

CALLE NUEVA UNO SUR

ESQUEMA TIPO UBICACION
DE LA CASETA SANITARIA
EN EL TERRENO.

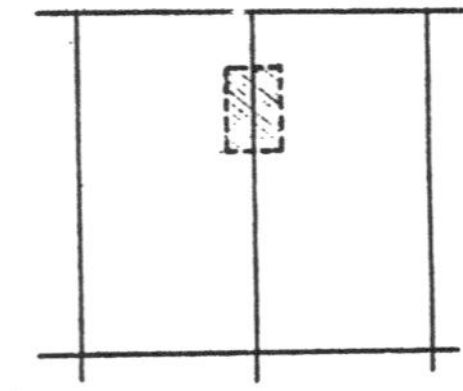

SIMBOLOGIA

MB	madera buen estado
MR	madera regular estado
MM	madera mal estado
	vivienda que se reubica 204
Ⓝ	lote que se crea para reubicar vivienda 132

Preparing and presenting the first exercise

After returning to the classroom, members discuss their findings within the groups. The two large sheets are used for their presentations, one for the problems, the other for the opportunities. Identification is analyzed under three headings: What? Why? and For Whom?

The workshop leader encourages the recording of all observations; but as time progresses, information is qualified by group discussion before it is written on the sheets. Participants debate their views, so that the identification and evaluation of issues is subject to everyone's consideration.

After the sheets are finished, they are taped to the wall and presented to the entire workshop. Emphasis is placed on the clarification of existing issues, not on future actions. Each group answers questions at the end of its presentation so that the understanding of problems and opportunities is made explicit to everyone.

¿QUE' BUENAS MALAS	2 ¿PORQUE'? ¿POR QUÉ ES UN PROBLEMA?	¿PARA QUIÉN? ES UN PROBLEMA
BUENAS		
1. TENER UN SITIO (1)	→ PARA LA FAMILIA Y EN ESPECIAL POR LOS NIÑOS	PARA TODOS
2. TENER CASETA. (2) – AGUA – ELECTRICIDAD – ALCANTARILLADO		PARA TODOS
3. TENER PLANO "TIPO" PARA CONSTRUIR CASA (MUNIC)	→ ASESORÍA PARA CONSTRUIR	
4. ARBORIZACIÓN		
5. SOLERAS Y SOLERILLAS	→ ORDENAN CIRCULACIÓN Y ARBORIZACIÓN	
6. MULTICANCHA "PROVISORIA"		
7. TENER AREAS VERDES POTENCIALES (EL ESPACIO Y LOS ARREGLOS QUE SE HAN HECHO)		
8. EXTRACCIÓN DE BASURAS (3)		PARA TODOS
9. PASAJES BUENOS POR SER ANCHOS.		
10. TENER "FERIA LIBRE CERCA"		
11. BUENA MOVILIZACIÓN		
12. EXISTE POLICLINICO		
13. BUENA DOTACIÓN DE COLEGIOS Y GUARDERÍAS.		
14. QUE SE HAYAN OTORGADO PATENTES PROVISORIAS COMERCIALES		
15. QUE SE ESTÉ EN PROCESO DE OTORGAMIENTO DE TITULOS DE PROPIEDAD.		
16. PAVIMENTACIÓN BALDOMERO LILLO		
17. REFUGIOS EN PARADEROS DE LOCOMOCIÓN		
18. EXISTENCIA JUNTA DE VECINOS		
19. ORGANIZACIÓN Y ATENCIÓN POR PARTE DE LA MUNICIPALIDAD.—		

Prioritizing problems and opportunities

The groups reassemble after a short coffee break. The workshop leader asks that each group discuss the problems and opportunities they have recorded and rank them by importance. He explains that resources are likely to be limited, and that a priority for improvements is best established through consensus. Each group is to number the top three issues in each category.

One group debates what is the greater problem: the level of unemployment or the rate of crime? An older resident from the settlement offers her argument and finds agreement: unemployment is the more critical; when jobs are found there will no longer be a problem with crime.

Each group presents to the full workshop. Discussion consists of a variety of doubt and agreement, experience and opinion. Most issues attract interest, clarified by the technical knowledge of some or the practical understanding of others. One issue is resolved by its lack of support; the problem is identified as affecting a small portion of the settlement, and is dismissed as less important than others.

The workshop leader follows the presentations with his observations. Some selections overlap: they have been identified independently, but actually stress the same concern. Another issue remains particularly tricky; it is a problem to some, but an opportunity to others. He explains that the workshop has identified and ordered the issues — good and bad — through the participants' consensus. Resolving these issues, by comparing improvement strategies and their trade-offs will be the next exercise.

Identifying strategies for improvement

The second session begins with an explanation of its two exercises: the first will identify the approaches that might be used in improving local conditions; the second will evaluate these potential strategies by comparing their trade-offs (cost, time-frame, etc.).

The previous groups are reshuffled. Participants again count off by threes; the workshop leader sees that each group has a facilitator and a few of the more outspoken members from the previous session. He explains that each new sheet will hold the analysis of a single problem. Three columns are to be filled. The first column will list optional approaches for improvement. Corresponding to each approach in the second column: who will carry this out? And in the third column: What would they do? What are the specific actions?

1 VIGILANCIA
GRUPO 3
OPCIONES
QUIÉN
CÓMO
OBJETIVO.
ELIMINAR CLANDESTINAJE (BARES)
COMUNIDAD
MUNICIPALIDAD
CARABINEROS
DPTO. DE PATENTES
ÚLTIMA INSTANCIA
ii VIGILANCIA POLICIAL (DELINCUENCIA)
INVESTIGACIONES
SIST. DENUNCIAS
2. CESANTIA
¿QUIÉN?
¿CÓMO?
1. AUMENTO DE CUPOS DE PROGR. DE EMPLEO
MUNICIPIO
2. FOMENTAR CAPACITACIÓN DE LOS POBLADORES
CONVENIOS CON UNIVERSIDADES, INSTITUTOS, INACAP, ETC.

Each group is given two new sheets and asked to begin by selecting two problems from the prioritized lists of the previous session. Deciding on which problems to address plunges the new groups into immediate discussion.

The dynamics of group work

Dynamics within the groups change as work progresses. In newly formed groups, the most outspoken are the first to assert their views. The facilitators draw the others into discussion and take less of a part as others participate. Selection of the problems to be analysed takes about ten minutes — at which point there are few participants satisfied with a listening role.

The workshop leader pushes the groups along by asking which problem they are working on, and frowning at his watch. As before, information is recorded on the sheets only after debate and agreement. Options that lack a group's support are not shared with the entire workshop.

After about one hour, groups begin to tape up their finished sheets and take a cup of coffee. Those still working seem to realize the opportunity they are missing, so it is not long before all the sheets are posted. By the end of the break, participants are standing around the sheets and talking about them informally.

The dynamics of presentation

Two members present the first group's work. The first reads across the sheet horizontally: What is the approach? Who is involved? What specific actions are involved? The second member is a resident from the settlement and provides some local colour that places the group's ideas into a rich context. The workshop audience occasionally asks a clarifying question, until the presentation is complete and the presenters are applauded.

The physical arrangement of the people in the workshop now supplements presentation. Previously, translation to the workshop leaders in the front of the room (adjacent to the presentation) seemed to interrupt the exchange between speaker and audience. Now, because the rear wall is being used for presentation and the translation remains at the front of the room, there is a more direct communication.

Evaluating strategies for improvement

The workshop leader explains that the second exercise in this session evaluates the improvement strategies by comparing their trade-offs. He divides the settlement into five physical aspects — houses, public spaces, services, streets and green areas. Within each of these aspects, the groups must decide how their strategies for improvement would be implemented. Specifically, they are to answer on the sheets:

(1) What is the recommendation for improvement?
(2) What are the critical considerations? (who, when, where, etc.)
(3) What will it cost. How will it be paid for?

He explains the third is a part of the second, but because of the importance of limited resources, should be considered independently. This will enable the negotiation and balance of public and community investments.

The workshop leader stresses that the groups consider a variety of recommendations — both general and specific — long-term and immediate. All the previous work supplies a resource for this exercise. The intention is to build on what has already been established. He suggests they may want to divide within the groups to work on individual aspects. Sheets will be posted in one hour.

The groups turn inwards — the intensity of their discussions seems to make each group oblivious to the others.

Assessing the trade-offs

The third session follows lunch. A panel is assembled to evaluate the physical options prepared by each group. Five workshop members make up the panel; the head of the municipal planning department, an engineer who coordinates the municipal jobs programme, an official from the UN Human Settlements Department, the president of the settlement's social organization and an architect that co-ordinates the university's technical assistance office in another municipality. Each is asked to comment on the presentations in his official role. What are the implications of policy? How do these ideas fit?

The walls are covered with previous work, so these sheets have been taped to the windows. A member from each group presents to the panel. Discussion is controlled, the give and take of earlier presentations now emphasizes the panel's responses. The ideas of each group are evaluated by those with the responsibility to change.

At the close, the workshop's most outspoken participant asks if anything is going to happen now. The municipal official replies, 'Yes'.

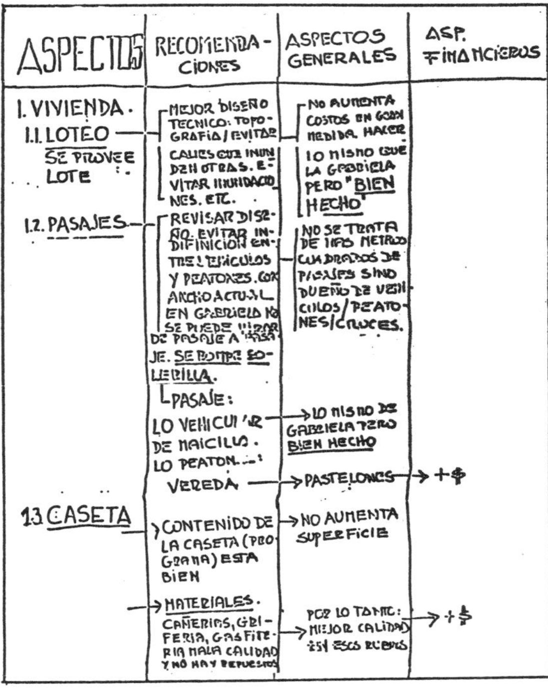

HOW THE OBJECTIVES WERE MET

The workshop at La Pintana brought together a variety of people — each involved in a different way with housing settlements. The agenda followed was based on the Microplanning approach. This analysis looks at how the workshop fits the objectives of the approach. Each objective is an important concern in settlement planning. Speed, participation and scale have been briefly explained, but will now be considered with the experiences of the workshop.

Speed, bridging study and action

The first objective of the Microplanning approach is speed. Rapid, practical results should be a part of every planning process. Planning for housing settlements can emphasize study, only to find that the corresponding actions of implementation do not work as anticipated. Were study and action bridged in the La Pintana workshop?

This assessment appears difficult. Ideas developed during the workshop have not had time to be implemented. Options that received popular support during the exercises may still prove unsuccessful in practice. It is too early to tell.

The suggestions from the workshop may also be weakened by the shortening of the agenda because of a national strike. Workshop leaders decided to delete an exercise that would have required participants to resolve government expenditure and community investment. In any case, the implementation of plans made during the workshop will have to be evaluated at a later time, a responsibility that remains largely with local participants.

The speed objective can be considered in a different light. While options developed at the workshop were not immediately implemented, the actions of earlier planners were under study. By identifying the problems of the existing settlement, participants had monitored the actions of previous interventions and incorporated those lessons in their options and strategies. It was not necessary to carry out extensive studies to evaluate past efforts. In fact, the initial field survey and the continued exchange of information between participants during the other exercises provided ample study for a number of planning actions to be put forth and evaluated.

An example helps to illustrate this point. Problems with electricity provision were cited from different viewpoints. Electric meters were commonly 'jumped' (bypassed) by residents, leaving the utility authorities with the opinion that customers were not paying on purpose, and that a much more expensive tamper-proof system would have to be installed. Residents, however, identified a different problem. The meters were burning out when the house's size grew and more electricity was needed so the occupants had jumped the meters to avoid being without electricity entirely. A strategy to alleviate both problems followed rather simply — install larger fuses in the meters. In this case, monitoring had informed planning from prior implementation, so the gap between study and action had been bridged.

Participation, working with diversity

The participation objective holds that settlement planning benefits from the greatest representation of interests. These interests are resolved collectively — participants working together in a series of negotiation aimed at the identification of meaningful problems and solutions. The workshop provides the meeting place, and the Microplanning approach sets the framework to guide the participants' interactions. At the La Pintana workshop, invited members of the central ministries and some local residents chose not to participate. How did this affect the objective of participation: did diverse interests work together for settlement improvements?

The workshop leaders had intended to divide the participants by expertise — settlement residents, government officials and technical professionals would each form their own group. The exercises of the first session would identify and prioritize the problems/opportunities within these groups. Resolution of their findings would follow in an open discussion directed by the workshop leader. Issues would be listed by agreement: if two or three of the groups had the same problem, it would be placed on a summary list. If an issue was identified by only one group, they would have the chance to convince at least one other group of its importance. The summary list would represent a final consensus.

The second session would begin with the top two or three problems. Residents would form three groups with technical professionals acting as advisors to identify and evaluate strategies for improvement. In the final session a panel of government officials would respond to these findings and highlight any general lessons that related to policy implementation.

If the participation objective requires a particular variety of participants, then the results from the workshop are uncertain. The anticipated agenda proved unworkable when there were not enough government officials to form a group. Instead, each group was assembled with a mix of settlement residents, government officials and technical professionals. If the members of the ministries are needed to effect change, the implementation of the workshop's suggestions is in doubt.

Results may be misdirected if local participants do not represent the community accurately. Representation seemed diverse, although some people had said they would not be able to come because their viewpoints were too divergent to make attendance comfortable. They might have provided a broader range of ideas in each of the exercises — a quality that is central to the participation objective. It is also possible that they would have played a disruptive role, although this seems unlikely given the wide range of interests represented and the constructive dynamics that were observed. Assembling the 'correct' variety of participants, so as to facilitate the greatest representation of interests, remains an uncertain issue in the evaluation of the participation objective.

The Microplanning approach provided the framework to enable participants to work together. Procedures in the workshop were adjusted for a different mix of participants than had been expected. Combining residents, officials and professionals in each group proved successful. Interactions that began with the simple folding of presentation sheets were developed into an open forum where individual opinions were heard. Even the most outspoken took their turn; resident, minister, official and school teacher each made different points and enjoyed the opportunity to be heard by an attentive audience focused on change.

Participation at the workshop can be considered in two ways: attendance and interaction. In the first, a diverse mix of participants are relied upon to supply an appropriate set of interests. Certain participants may be required for the resolution of certain issues. Without them, necessary interests may not be represented, and the results that follow may be misdirected or abandoned before final implementation. Identifying the range of interests and ensuring their attendance is a responsibility that lies more with the individual participants than anyone else.

In the second way, participation aims to ensure meaningful results through the interaction of participants. All that attend must be encouraged to take part in an open exchange of ideas if diverse interests are to be spoken, heard and assembled constructively. The sessions succeeded in bringing different people together and enabling them to work side by side. The workshop provided a meeting place and an approach for interaction between those involved with the planning of settlement improvements in La Pintana.

Scale, a progression of effects

The objective of scale involves progression.

The Microplanning approach has been used before to train planners involved with new settlements and upgrading. Teaching one group of people so that they can train others has allowed the effects of a single workshop to progress rapidly. Is the objective of scale appropriate for the La Pintana workshop?

The workshop at La Pintana was not intended to train planners. It was a demonstration project seeded by limited research funds; the intention was to explore a coalition of interests in establishing a continuing settlement improvement programme in Chile. The participants included those from the universities and government who may want to organize additional workshops, but it also included those from the local community who were interested more in physical results and the opportunity to be part of the decision-making process. Within this context, the objective of scale was met.

Each participant involved in the workshop bargained for results based upon their individual interests. Interests may be satisfied in several ways. As has been discussed in the last section, the nature of the Microplanning approach is participatory. This participation does not ensure that an ideally balanced set of interests are in attendance, but once present, it supports the resolution of divergent issues through participant interaction. Implemented actions will be the result of negotiations that require the voluntary agreement of attendant interests.

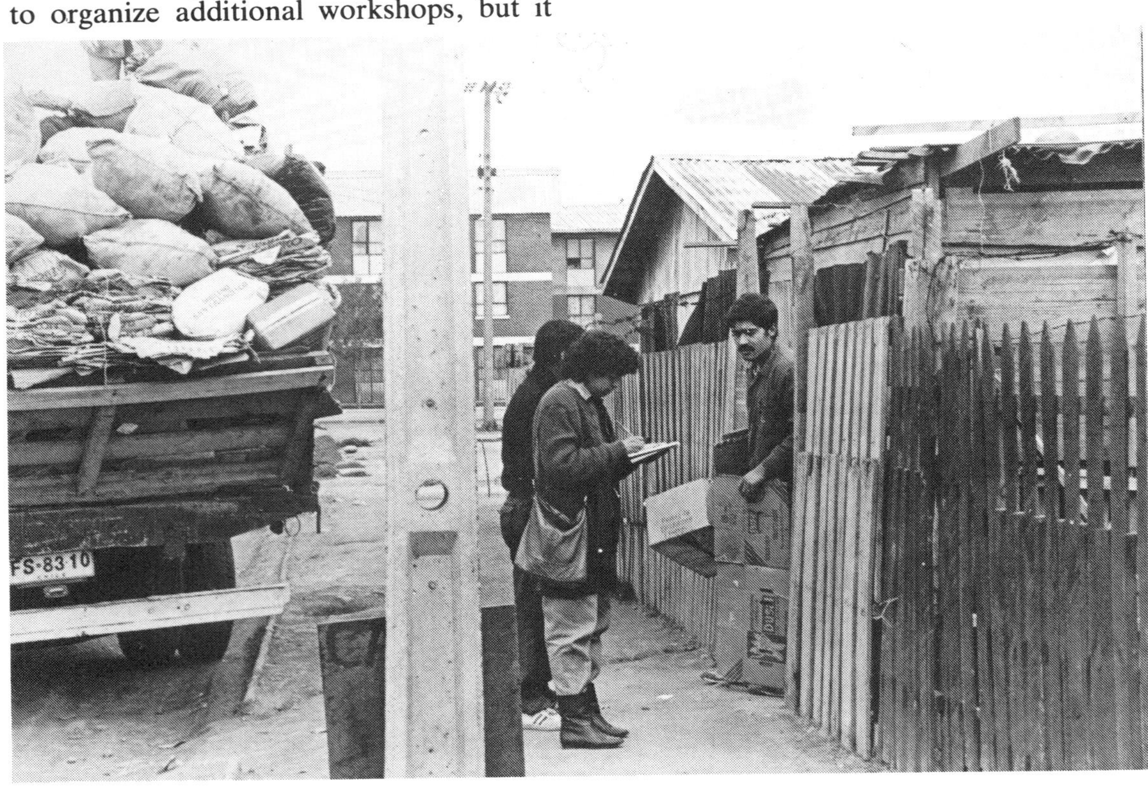

The satisfaction of settlement residents may depend upon the plans that are finally implemented. As discussed in the section on speed, practical results are the continuing responsibility of local participants. For several, physical actions remain the measuring stick with which the success of the workshop will be judged. If physical improvements follow, the interests of these local participants will be met, and their participation and support of later planning efforts are likely to continue to influence others in ther community.

A similar progression can be imagined for those participants from the more centralized institutions. Each expects different results from the workshop — this publication is only one example. If their interests are satisfied, planning efforts may progress to include more workshops, publications and research projects.

The progression of scale will depend upon the different ways in which results are interpreted by participants. From the local level to the more central, participants will be seeking their own satisfaction. Whether a physical improvement to the settlement, or the sharing of ideas with others, the objective of scale will succeed if participants recognize the benefits of a participatory approach and are willing to explore it with others. In the best case, the objective means a growing awareness of the co-operation that is possible between those with different interests.

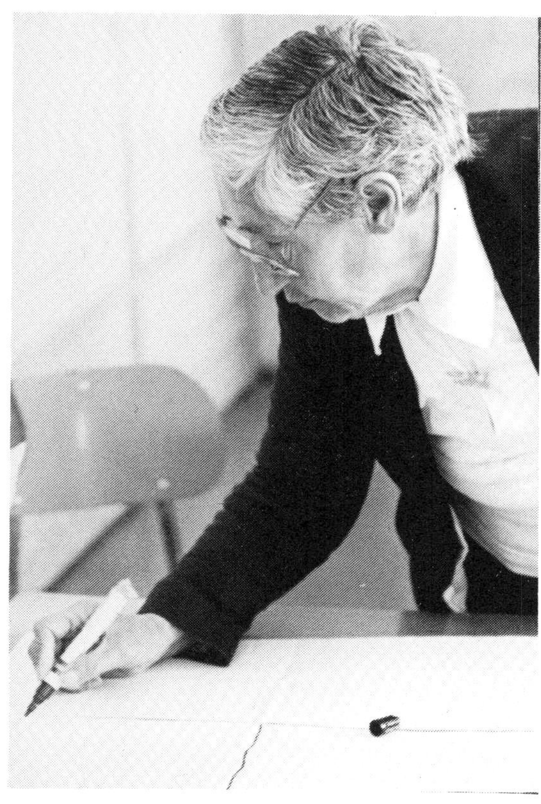

3. LEARNING FROM IMPLEMENTATION

CASES IN SRI LANKA

INTRODUCTION

In the course of the month of January, 1987, I had the opportunity of surveying four of the dozen or so community development projects that have been undertaken by Sri Lanka's National Housing Development Authority (NHDA) in the last four years under the 'Micro Level Social Planning' scheme. This scheme advocates the direct participation of communities in a process that comprises the definition of their main environmental and physical deficiencies and problems, of the required actions or solutions, of the required resources and time for implementing such solutions, and of the different agents that become responsible for the implementation of such solutions within the established schedule. In short, this programme puts the concept of Microplanning into practice.

THE WORKSHOP AND ITS ACTORS

The main activity and starting point in this process is an intense two- to three-day workshop held on-site with the participation of the community through their representatives (the Community Development Council, or CDC; and within this, a hierarchical body or Committee: the CDCC); the NHDA's representatives (and among these, the Project Officer, or PO, who plays a primary role throughout the project in the general organization of information and meetings, in the supervision of the project's progress and by mediating between the community and other agents); representatives of the district's Municipal Council (health officers, engineers, land surveyors, etc.) and representatives of foreign or private donors and funding agencies (non-governmental organizations, or NGOs).

These workshops and the concept of Microplanning were recently introduced with support from MIT faculty. This is part of on-going assistance to the government's programme of minimizing direct intervention while implementing a vast upgrading programme aimed at low income settlers in both urban and rural areas.

OBJECTIVES OF THIS SECTION

New as it is, this is a live process, feeding on experience; the workshop procedures and the author's understanding of the workshop's purpose have had a mostly pragmatic evolution. Although still in a trial stage, the straightforwardness of the operations and the rather encouraging results already seem to suggest the possibility of an ambitious leap towards a much more comprehensive, large-scale development programme to be applied throughout the nation.

It is for this purpose, however, that the observations concentrate on the most relevant and variable of the Microplanning stages and perhaps the least judged yet: that of the process of actual implementation of the workshop's outcome as they have been described above.

It is not intended to evaluate and judge the methods, their application, or the theory behind them; we have by now a fair idea of the benefits and potentials of Microplanning in its first stages. We know that it articulates priorities, and that it 'performs' — delivering self-consciousness and confidence — and mobilizes the communities constructively. Instead, the focus is on the way the whole process develops over time after these methods have been applied.

Rather than an inward view, this is intended to be an outward one, that of the external, unexpected and rather uncontrollable agents that affect the development of the Microplanning and that must be dealt with in order to act quickly and successfully. We must answer questions such as what the most common administrative bottlenecks are, what the participants' points of view are and how good communications are among the participants, how well expectations are met, whether resources are available or properly allocated, and so on. Our ultimate goal is to detect what must be improved and how, in order to modify procedures, methods and theories aimed at large-scale implementation programmes.

THE COMMUNITIES INVOLVED

Of the four sites visited, one — Moratuwa — is located in a rural area 12 miles from the city of Colombo; the other three are within the Colombo Municipal Council (CMC) limits and are of clear urban character. These four communities are quite different from each other; however, in each case a workshop was held and a NHDA project officer is currently working with the community.

Between the 1 January and 19 January, 1987, I was able to gather equivalent information for each project, allowing eventual comparison and extrapolation. I was given a summary of the workshop's outcome for each case, plans of the original situation and of the proposed modifications. I visited and photographed each site, interviewed the CDC members, the POs involved and other officials as well as agents from other organizations.

Sebastian Gray

CASE STUDIES

PROJECT: GOTHAMI ROAD

DATE OF WORKSHOP: 14–15 JUNE 1985

UNITS: 212

FAMILIES: 250

Gothami Road, in a quarter of Colombo called Borella, is a parcel of State-owned land bordered by a canal, private land and some NHDA apartment blocks. Families squatted here and developed a settlement in what is mostly lowland or marsh and thus rather depreciated land. The project has been divided into two sections to deal with the dual nature of the site: the first being the most coherent morphologically (a single linear path with dwellings arranged about it) and with the best environmental conditions; the second being the one where most of the lowlands are, presenting greater difficulty and cost for upgrading. A high-tension line crosses part of the project.

This project falls under the category of Low-income Housing Improvement Project Areas, formally declared so within specified boundaries, a status that legally allows and demands from the NHDA the funding of physical improvements.

This was the first Microplanning workshop.

The following is a reproduction of the workshop's outcome and agreed-upon activities or solutions, followed by a more comprehensive analysis based on on-field observations and an interview with 7 of the 17 CDCC members including their president. It was also possible to speak to NHDA's Land Officer.

PRIORITIES/ACTIVITIES

1. Drains and earth-filling
(a) Repair existing drains
(b) Construct new drains
(c) Raise foundations

2. Community Centre
(a) Use open space
(b) Construct a new building
(c) Construct a temporary building
(d) Meet under the big tree

3. Repairing existing houses
(a) Get technical knowledge for self-help
(b) Get NHDA loans
(c) Get building materials
(d) Contract labour
(e) Organize co-operative system
(f) Get bank loans

4. Health information
(a) Door-to-door advice (by the CMC Health Wardens)
(b) Lectures
(c) Posters, handbills
(d) Informal discussions
(e) Training of some community members as advisers
(f) Community drama shop
(g) Puppet show
(h) Films, videos

5. Street lighting
(a) Contact the CMC
(b) Collect money from community members
(c) Find donors

6. Toilets
(a) Repair existing latrines
(b) Build new latrines
(c) Build individual toilets
(d) Build common/private toilets

7. Adult education
(a) Identify needs, illiterate
(b) Use existing facilities
(c) Get tools, methods, materials
(d) Train

8. Repair water lines
(a) Get necessary infrastructure and materials for self-repairing
(b) Inform government
(c) Contract labour
(d) Organize community construction committee
(e) Get technical advice from the NHDA

9. Land tenure
(a) Buy land at reasonable rate
(b) Get a long-term lease
(c) Get freehold of land
(d) Get long-term instalments

1. Earth-Filling and Construction of Drains

Status: On-going.
Description: This task is undertaken by the NHDA; the community has agreed to provide an important part of the necessary labour.

The NHDA contracts the Colombo Commercial Company, a semi-private enterprise, which in turn subcontracts a private enterprise to supply loose earth at the site. The actual spreading of the earth is done with tools and labour provided by the community, through *Sramadana* (volunteer works). The CDC has agreed that each household should buy a bucket. NHDA's officers supervise filling levels given by NHDA's technical commission. Most houses already have raised plinths to prevent the usual flooding during rainy seasons; however, some people will spread earth on the house floors. The Engineer division of the NHDA is responsible for calculating the quality and volume of needed filling-earth in both stages. The filling of the first stage started in November 1986, with the arrival of a new project officer; that is, a year and five months after completion of the workshop.

PO (Project Officer): The supply of earth on site has been very irregular; because of the conditions described, trucks get stuck in the mud, slowing the operation down to one load a day. The NHDA/ contractor/subcontractor link makes communication and complaints more difficult; in fact, NHDA's Engineering Division has complained to the contractor several times with little result. Filling-earth is left on the main road to be carried and spread out in the backyards by means of volunteer works. There is an evident scarcity of appropriate tools (there are a couple of wheelbarrows) aggravated by the fact that most are shared on a basis of personal relationship rather than freely throughout the community.

All definitive earth-drains (ditches) will be excavated after the filling. Cement-drains will be built along the main road only. Five houses in the first stage had to be rebuilt according to the blocking-out plan in order to meet the new ground level.

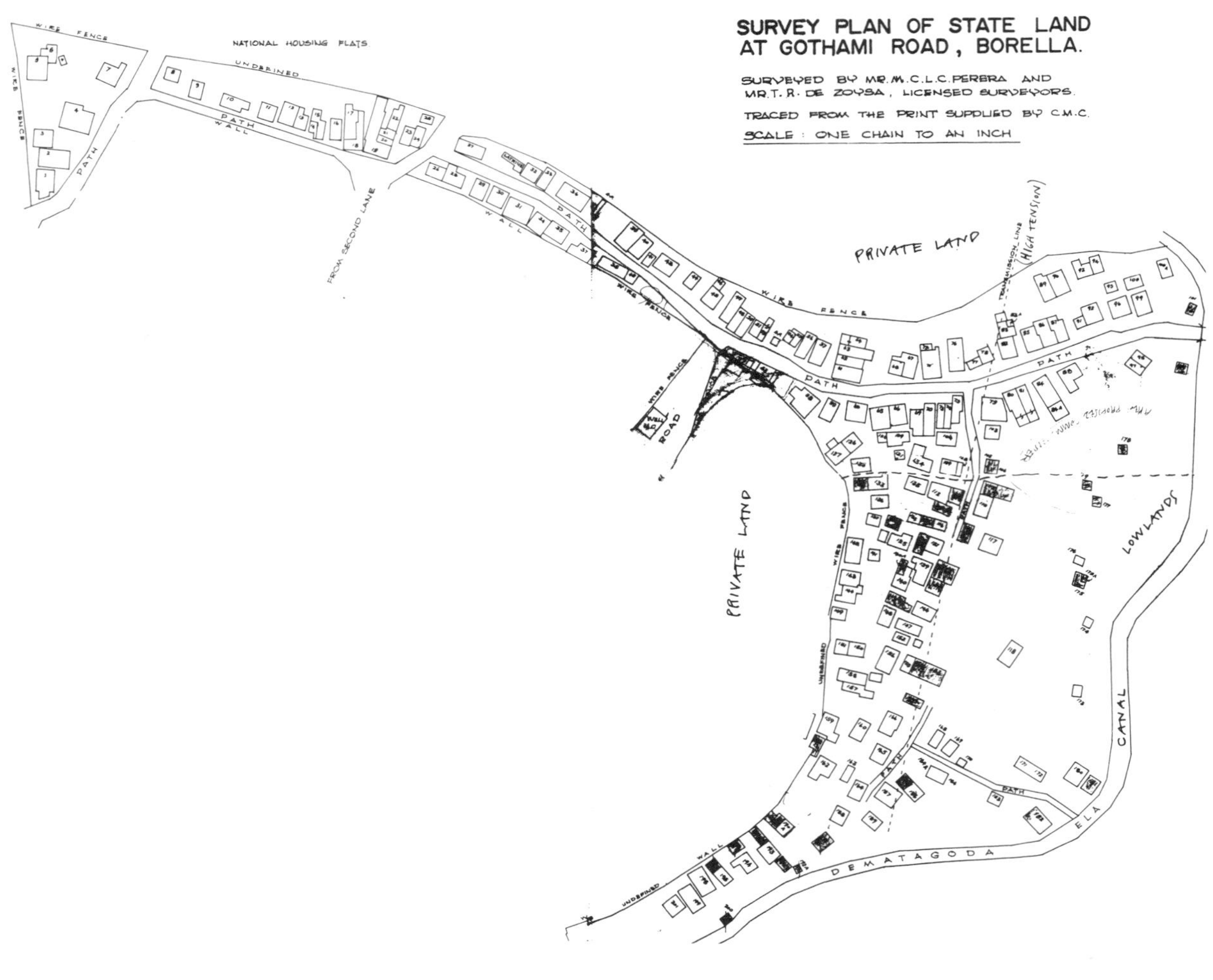

CDC: The community cannot supply all the needed labour: the *Sramadana* are not enough since the only spare time they have is holidays and evenings. The main difficulty is in carrying the earth from the entrance of the project site (where it is left by the trucks) to the most distant lots. Tools were not supplied and 'not everyone got tools' in the words of a community member. However, the earth has been supplied very slowly (the subcontractor uses small vehicles in order to get through on the narrow roads), so they have managed so far. The average amount of earth carried a day is ten cubes.

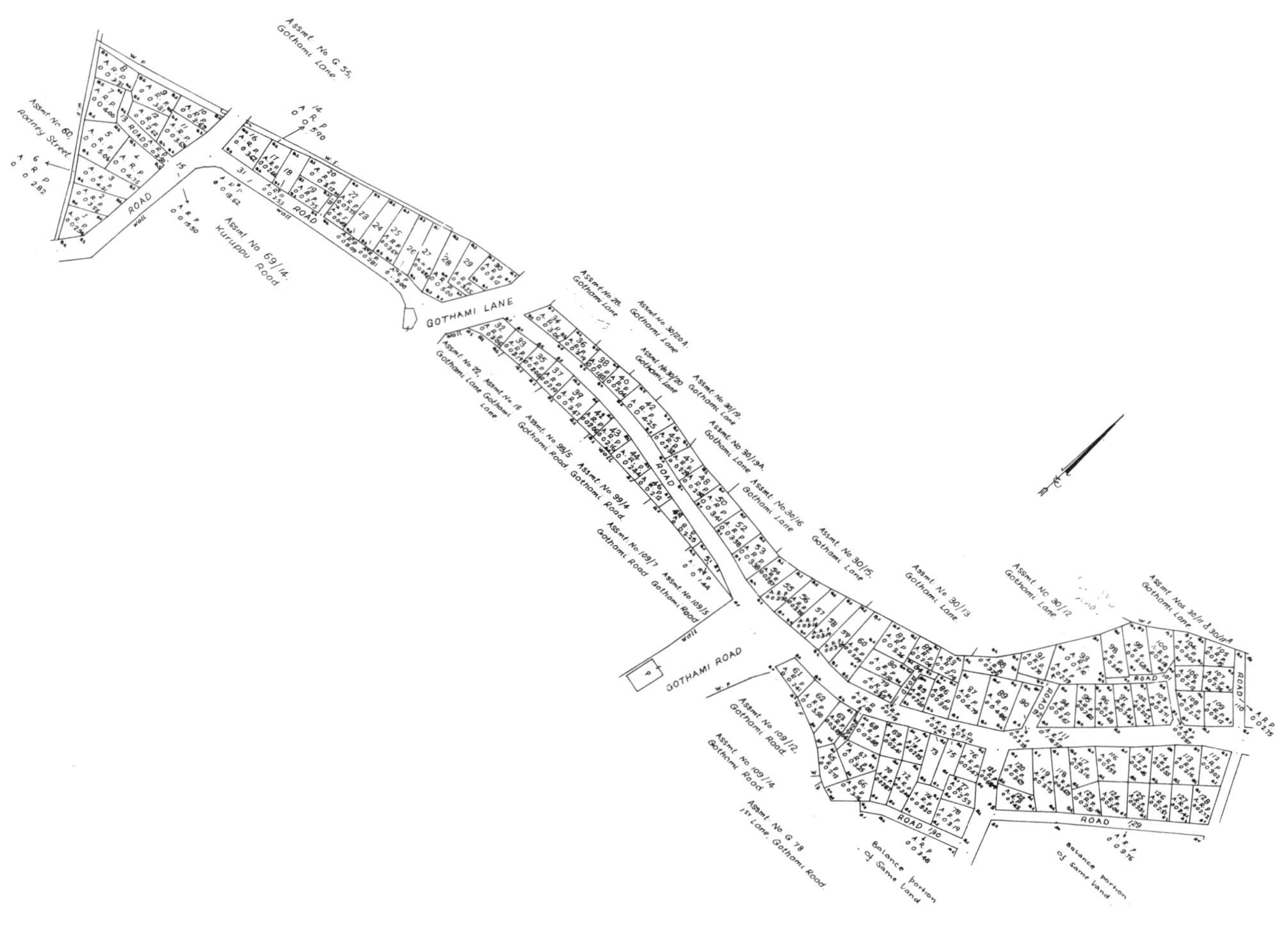

COMMENTS

Although in this case the community evaluated earth-filling and the installation of proper drains as the first priority, other necessarily antecedent activities such as the blocking-out (layout regularization, redistribution of land in more homogeneous lots according to surveys and plans by the NHDA) were not taken into consideration. In fact, blocking-out does not appear as a single priority at all in the workshop outcome, although it was among the first activities to be carefully planned and currently carried out in the first stage after the workshop (but not without delays, as I will describe further on). Subsequent workshops considered blocking-out among the first priorities or activities.

The arrival of a new Project Officer was also significant. POs are very much involved with the community, they play a delicate role in which they bear the hopes, confidence and frustrations of many families; they get to manage a vast amount of information and rather subjective but valuable details regarding individual behaviour, relationships, resources and the like. It is unfortunate in this process that a PO should be replaced in the sense that continuity is lost that takes time to recover.

It was agreed at the time of the workshop that tools would not be supplied and that the community would see that each household acquired some. What seemed a reasonable commitment proved hard to carry out in reality; the community members seemed unable or reluctant to invest in tools in spite of the evident need and benefit. The explanation may be found in the fact that, as noted, earth had been supplied very slowly and therefore there was not a need for better organization or more intensive work. It is worth noting that the slow pace seemed well suited to the available time and other resources of the community; one wonders what the dynamics would have been if pressed by prompt and voluminous deliveries of earth, everyone had bought or borrowed the needed tools; whether time-shifts would have been organized and how well all this would have gone. One also wonders whether this should not have been considered as a slow task indeed, a major task previous even to the workshop.

Although recommended by NHDA's Engineering Department, the soil used for the filling of marshes seemed rather unsuitable: it was very impermeable, clayish and without gravel; the rains rendered it muddy and hard to drain.

2. A COMMUNITY CENTRE

Status: Not implemented.
Description: A physical place for meetings and other community-oriented activities such as child care, mobile clinics, etc.

After the workshop, a temporary structure was built as a pre-school and is still in use. Land has been allocated in the blocking-out plan for a community hall on the second stage area, which will not be developed until the first stage is completed. General meetings have been held at a nearby Buddhist temple on Gothami Road; it has been proposed to make more frequent and formal use of this facility.

PO: The community is allowed to use the mentioned temple and the rooms of a school a quarter of a mile distant. The existing temporary building houses a successful pre-school for which the CDC requested money and help from the CMC's Health Warden. It also houses meetings of the Thrift and Credit Society and of other community matters. The construction and furnishings were funded by UNICEF and private donors.

CDC: The community has agreed on the future location of the definitive community hall; the chosen site is central and non-conflictive.

3. REPAIRING THE EXISTING HOUSES

Status: Not implemented.
Description: Before any actual upgrading of the dwellings is attempted, two operations must be completed: the first is that of the blocking-out, as it was defined previously.

This regularization of the layout attempts the redistribution of land in relatively equal plots causing the least disturbance to the existing structures. Each house is given a 2.5 to 3 perch lot as a minimum (1 perch = 25 m^2 approx.). Larger lots are kept in exceptional cases; if there is more than one house in a 2.5 perch lot, one will be relocated in vacant lots within the same community, following a community's decision which is communicated to the NHDA in due time. Usually the oldest family in the original lot stays. In the case of Gothami Road, the land has been completely blocked-out and marked. Families will move to the new layout and will start constructing or upgrading their homes after the completion of the second operation, that is, the land-filling of the first stage, when small loans will be made available to each family through a Thrift and Credit Society (co-operative savings; the NHDA issues loans to the Thrift and Credit Society District Union, this issues to the local Thrift and Credit Societies which in turn offer loans to their communities). Families in the second stage will have to wait and join later. Although this is not very desirable, it is a way to get started without having to wait for the whole.

PO: No loans will be offered before the land-filling, to prevent possible misuse of the money. In order to be eligible, people have been requested to join the Thrift and Credit Society and deposit 10 per cent of the expected loan one year in advance; as of now ten families have completed. The CDC board is the same as in the Thrift and Credit Society; it meets once a month.

Some families have already upgraded their homes without the need of a loan.

CMC: Small repairs such as replacing planks, walls and decaying roofs were done individually after the workshop. In some cases labour was shared.

COMMENTS

There was a six-month delay in the survey of this site due to lack of personnel. The CMC, responsible for this task, was busy at that time surveying land for new facilities for the Kettearama Stadium — one of the Prime Minister's pet projects — right before the Asian Cup (a cricket competition) was held in April, 1986. The PO complained to the CMC personally every week, but the CMC surveys by contract from the NHDA and apparently 'the payments were unclear,' which may account for the half-year negligence just as well.

14. HEALTH INFORMATION

Status: On-going.
Description: Most health-related issues and activites in this type of community are the responsibility of the local Municipal Council's Health Warden; in this case, the

CMC: Its programme basically consists of education and consciousness-raising, immunization and the eventual training of some community members to become health monitors.

PO: The current officer is not informed of the degree of implementation of the health programme; he perceives it as being 'not very important in this case' and thinks it has not been implemented yet.

CDC: The community members do not recognize a currently on-going health programme. They rather recall distinct activities undertaken by the CMC's Health Warden which correspond to the Microplan: there were a puppet show, films, first-aid lectures, the CMC surveyed the population twice, gave some advice and immunization, trained two people and supplied them with first-aid boxes. The CDC members declared they were satisfied.

COMMENTS

The perception of the PO may be explained by the fact that he is new to the project and not thoroughly familiarized with it from its beginning. Perhaps more significant, this may be due to the fact that the CMC is a body that operates independently from the NHDA and that in general these two organizations have few opportunities of communication or feedback. The CMC is experienced and efficient in dealing with health issues; the NHDA's workshop serves its purpose in pointing out the main needs for the CMC to take care of.

5. STREET LIGHTING

Status: Not implemented.
Description: There is no lighting in the public circulation areas; it is desirable particularly along the main road and paths. The installation of standard public lighting is expensive and requires qualified labour; it seems that there is little the community can do on its own initiative. This is a service to be provided by the authority.

PO: After the land-filling and blocking-out, the NHDA will request the CMC or the Electricity Board to prepare a proposal and budget according to the technical data supplied (that is, the regularized layout). The CMC or Electricity Board will then send a project back to the NHDA for approval and contract. If the CMC is to be chosen, it will in turn subcontract a private firm (as in the case of the supply of filling-earth described above).

CDC: Waiting for the land-filling, blocking out.

COMMENTS

Due to its technical aspects, carrying out this priority seems rather out of the control of the community. Although important, it belongs in the category of priorities that must necessarily wait until the main operations are completed. It is possible to note already that setting priorities should conciliate the needs and desires of the community, the available resources and an implementation strategy. This strategy could have the form of a critical path diagram which should be made graphically clear to the community. Anxieties, frustrations or a sense of negligence could be avoided by realizing the current stage of development and the relative position and order of the actions and implementations.

6. TOILETS

Status: Not implemented.
Description: The existing common sanitary services are insufficient and in very

poor condition. Due to the vicinity of the canal and to the poor quality of the ground, there is a very high water table (6ft. approx.), and pit-latrines cannot be constructed. Large septic tanks are used instead; these are periodically emptied by the CMC — although evidently not as often as necessary — because they are placed below the level of possible connection to the existing sewerage lines.

PO: The blocking-out provides space for new common toilet blocks. The location for the new blocks was decided by agreement with the CDC members and according to the location of the existing latrines. No new toilet blocks will be built until after the land-filling is completed. However, the CDC requested a self-built temporary toilet block from the NHDA, if materials and assistance were provided. The PO selected a lot in December 1986, and requested the necessary plans from NHDA's Technical Officer. As of the time of this survey, the temporary block's budget and plans were in the process of approval by NHDA's Chairman. Once approved, the community will receive cash money and plans plus on-site technical assistance; and they will self-build by means of volunteer works. The temporary toilet block will be located in stage II, partly to show some tangible progress to that part of the community.

CDC: The community did not repair the existing latrines; they had asked the CMC to empty the septic tanks in order to repair, but this was not done. The CDC's Treasurer went three times to the area's CMC to complain personally. The new toilet block will be built on a contract basis by the CDC/Thrift and Credit Society, but in order for the Thrift and Credit Society to exist and operate it is required that each member of the community makes a previous deposit. This process was slow; it was completed two weeks before the time of this survey.

Individual (private) toilets may be built when the house-improvement plan starts. So far, two newly built houses include individual toilets.

COMMENTS

No matter how 'temporary' a toilet block, it is likely to remain in use as long as possible. One toilet block, built at an early stage, will probably relieve the most immediate needs of the community (or at least a part of it). This leads us to the fact that, in addition to the concept of critical path, perhaps some of the solutions (activities, operations) must be broken down to smaller bits so that they can be implemented in a given period of time according to their own internal priorities: 'We need four new toilet blocks? Well, we'll build one right at the beginning while we wait for everything to be settled before we build the rest.' It is not a question of emergency solutions as much as a question of finding a satisfactory short-term partial solution as a way to start.

Again, in this case, the blocking-out was an initial step. Indeed, it is invariably an initial step for whatever physical improvements, so it could be considered a requisite even prior to the workshop, avoiding the discontinuity that the land-surveying/design/land-demarcating process produces between planning and action.

Another recurring problem is that informal communities have no legal recognition until the land-tenure process is completed, which often means being neglected by the municipal departments such as those of garbage collection, septic tank emptying, etc. It seems that at times the CMC acts only under the pressure of the NHDA officials. Perhaps it could be possible to create legal provisions for an intermediate state, in the way temporary deeds are to the land-tenure process.

7. ADULT EDUCATION

Status: On-going.
Description: This priority fulfills the concerns of the community regarding school drop-outs, unemployment, drug-addiction, illiteracy.

PO: Not informed. The officer believes that the community has been properly helped by the CMC.
CDC: Members of the CDC surveyed their own community. It was found that there were about 20 school drop-outs between ages 9 and 16, of both sexes. The CDC committee had evening classes arranged for the group at a nearby school: the classes consist of writing and reading and self-employment (informal income-generating) activities.

COMMENTS

As in previous items, it may be said on behalf of the PO that he is not completely familiar with the project from its beginning and that he is not necessarily responsible for every activity.

It would be advisable to keep a logbook of sorts so as to record the progress of each priority; this would have allowed the in-coming PO to be informed of the details of the project's history. Indeed such a book could have a standard form and be kept simultaneously by the CDC and the NHDA. This would not be confused with the book that each CDC currently keeps for the recording of meetings, visits, etc. If properly designed, this proposed logbook could become a useful organizational tool in the case of a large-scale programme, and also useful for statistic and evaluation purposes.

It is clear from this case that priorities can be divided into three major groups. In the first group are the very urgent and elementary priorities, usually related to the physical environment and legal issues involving the community as a single entity. These are usually the most expensive and slowest to implement: land-tenure, blocking-out and earth-filling. In the second group are the strongly needed and desired but less urgent provision of services. Although these are not the most expensive, they are still slow to implement because of the bureaucracy involved. These include water, street-lights, toilets, drains, garbage-collection. In the third group are the less immediate, group-issues. These are usually easier to carry out, for the necessary administrative framework is already there: pre-school, health, behaviour, unemployment, technical assistance, etc. Solutions to the most immediate priorities are almost always the hardest to implement. This fact is clearly not understood by the community and may lead to confusion, misunderstanding and frustration. This fact must be explicitly dealt with at the time of the workshop, either by producing a critical path diagram as proposed above, or by undertaking some of the main priorities ('basic actions'?) prior and out of the context of the workshop, as if preparing the field for an efficient community-managed process. The very fact that in this case the community organized and acted promptly and successfully supports this observation. In other words, Microplanning must deal realistically and creatively with those priorities that the community is best able to manage by itself. It should tend to exclude (from the workshop, not from the process) the actions that are out of its reach. These are recurrent top priorities that can be systematically dealt with by the authority in conjunction, whenever necessary, with the community, before the workshop takes place.

8. REPAIR WATER LINES

Status: On-going.
Description: Maintenance of the common water taps (drinking water) and common wells (for bathing and washing).
PO: Taps were repaired during March and April 1986. One is damaged again. There are about four taps for drinking water and 10 or 12 wells for bathing and washing. The community is generally responsible for the maintenance of the water taps, although some will have to be rebuilt (relocated or improved) after completion of the blocking-out.
CDC: The community has repaired the water taps three times since the workshop. There is an informal assignment for those who use a specific tap in order to collect money for repairs.

9. LAND TENURE

Status: On-going
Description: As it was mentioned before, a Thrift and Credit Society has been formed in this community to allow acquisition of the land and improvements of the dwellings. Small loans are made available only after a year of constitution and after each member has deposited 10 per cent of the expected loan.
PO: The year-old Thrift and Credit Society has 275 registered members and a Rs.89,000 fund. A Women's Committee was organized to start income-generating activities such as orchards and confectionery. Small monthly loans of Rs.100 ($4) are already available as introductory to the system. The complexity of the procedures and alternatives demands a slow development; different options are added every 3 or 4 months.

This land has been owned by the government; the CMC transferred it to the Department of Slum Improvements of the Urban Development Authority (UDA). This Department eventually became the NHDA; the UDA transferred the land to the NHDA in 1985. Although Stage I is blocked-out, no permanent deeds will be given until after the dwelling improvements are completed (that is, until after loans are given and three instalments paid back). If requested, temporary deeds may be given at this stage; these temporary deeds are an agreement for definitive deeds after the completion of repairs. Fifteen-year loans are for a 30-year lease. Stage II's loan programme will start after Stage I's is going on.

CDC: The community is aware of the procedures. Delays in getting loans were due to the terms of constitution of the Thrift and Credit Society: 10 per cent deposit, regular meetings, etc.

PROJECT: MORATUWA

DATE OF WORKSHOP: November 16–17, 1985

UNITS: 160

Moratuwa is located 12 miles away from Colombo; a railway separates the site from the beach. This community is physically and culturally related to the sea; it started as a well-organized informal settlement of fishermen, but included other groups as well.

Although land tenure has been regularized, this community is separated into two parts by a large parcel of privately-owned land that the NHDA tried unsuccessfully to purchase. Clearly, the improvements that occur in this settlement will raise the private land's value.

Moratuwa was among the first Microplanning workshops and among the first semi-rural areas in the Microplanning programme. At its earlier stage, the workshop followed a somewhat complex method of assessment of nominal amounts of money for each possible solution to the priority problems, exercises that were not fully understood and were regarded with suspicion 'as mere paperwork' by the community. There were also three groups formed to focus on different sets of priorities (community, health and technical), but each group produced a long list of problems upon which it was difficult to agree in the end. However, the workshop succeeded in problem identification and in bringing the community together in action and organization. Indeed, this appears to be one of the most successful cases of the Microplanning, community-involvement programme.

Participating agents are the NHDA through its District Manager and Area Project Officer, the Urban Council of Moratuwa (UC), and UNICEF, which has funded most amenities except electricity and the tarring of the roads.

Three CDC members were interviewed, including their president, who is politically active at the local level and exerts a certain influence on the settlement. It was also possible to talk to the Superintendent of Works of the Urban Council of Moratuwa.

PRIORITIES/SOLUTIONS

1. Housing
Clarify land ownership and secure housing loan from NHDA

2. Garbage disposal
Secure CDC participation

3. Drinking and bathing water
Build common wells and install a hand pump for drinking water (Government and CDC)

4. Toilets
Build individual toilets with advice and assistance from the NHDA (Government and CDC)

5. Pre-school
(a) Build a temporary building, start pre-school immediately
(b) Train teachers
(c) Get equipment (Government and CDC)

6. Health education
Select the better instructed to be trained by the UC Health Wardens (Government)

7. Community hall
Blocking-out should include a lot for it

8. School drop-outs and increasing income:
(a) Self-help (find alternative income-generating activities)
(b)Vocational training
(c) Get fishing equipment
(d)Identification of job-opportunity places
(e). Rationalize spendings

1. HOUSING

Status: On-going.
Description: Self-helped, self-built new house/upgrading programme with NHDA loans and technical assistance.

PO: The community was originally composed of 134 units, of which 25 were permanent. The blocking-out produced 160 plots of four perch each (1 perch = 25m^2 approx.), of which 134 were given to the 134 original settlers while the rest were allocated by the local Member of Parliament. The blocking-out was achieved in only five days with maximum community co-operation. Once all the land was allocated, NHDA loans for self-building were made available according to the families' income level (so as to help better those who are less resourceful while still ensuring capability of repayment): from Rs.8,000 to Rs. 15,000, to be given in four instalments proportional to the cost of the four main stages of construction (33.3 per cent for rough work from foundations up to the roof structure, 26.6 per cent for roofing, 20 per cent for carpentry and 20 per cent for finishes).

Of the 160, only five lots did not start construction of their houses, all of them belonging to outsiders who came to settle after the blocking-out.

Some members misused their loans and were not able to complete their construction: some houses were oversized or overdesigned. 'Some paid more attention to the mason and his interests (the more he builds, the more he earns) than to the technical officer,' said the PO. 'Others are just too lazy.'

Families usually hired one skilled labourer (a mason or a carpenter) for support; the rest was self-help.

CDC: The main problem is that some cannot complete their homes with the Rs.15,000 loans. Unfinished houses result mainly because some people have gone beyond the NHDA's instructions. 'They say: "Because a house is a house, and there'll be no second chance",' explains the CDC president. These people do not believe in the possibility of eventual expansions, despite NHDA's advice.

COMMENTS

The original plans presented by the NHDA were for two rooms, a separate kitchen and a toilet. Some added relatively large living rooms, integrated kitchen, porches, built-in closets and cupboards. Many houses have beautiful masonry and carpentry details.

Says the CDC president: 'Some people fear that they will lose their food stamps if they declare a better income,' which means that these got better loans to add to their own resources to the detriment of those who actually needed most help. These loans are intended to stimulate the community and encourage them to find other resources for the construction of their permanent homes. Many houses in this project show that this indeed has happened.

The community members expressed their wish that a much more detailed discussion of the essential priorities had taken place at the time of the workshop, that is, of housing improvement and loans. To some people, important things arose later that had not been well understood.

A key issue is that of miscalculation, enthusiasm, perhaps naiveté, that leads some people to embark on projects impossible to complete. In one case, a member of the community used his first instalment for a given business that would generate a profit. The business did not progress and, unable to achieve the first stage of construction, he did

not get further instalments and has not been able to continue. Emergencies, such as health problems, also translate into unexpected use of loans, usually slowing or stopping the process.

Should the workshop be more specific in the top priorities?
Should it allocate more time to these and less to the rest?
Should it be longer altogether, or be broken down into two or more sessions several months apart?

It is interesting to note that some of the 'outsiders' failed to get started. These came after the workshop, when the blocking-out had been completed. It is worth regarding these families as in need of special attention in order to have them effectively join the community and have a sense of integration and participation.

2. GARBAGE DISPOSAL

Status: Not implemented.
Description: Appropriate disposal of garbage, frequent collection.
PO: The UC built masonry bins and should collect periodically.
CDC: Collection of garbage will proceed when the roads are finished; meanwhile the community is dumping garbage on the beach, in special dumping areas, or burning it.

COMMENTS

Completion of roads appears here as a non-stated priority which is a pre-condition for effective garbage collection. Road layout is part of the blocking-out, but in order for trucks to come in to collect the garbage, roads have to be levelled and stabilized, which is in itself

a separate activity. This is again the question of critical path programming that could prevent unexpected delays and frustrations while allowing the community to do the kind of things that it is best prepared to do, such as finishing these roads.

3. WATER

Status: On-going.
Description: Provision of drinking and bathing/washing water.
PO: The project includes individual connections for drinking water. The NHDA is providing the network; each family must have its own connection and pipework done individually. Water for bathing and washing is provided at common facilities from wells built by the UC with UNICEF funds.
CDC: There is one drinking-water tap at the moment, at the site of the community centre. The existing wells are sufficient for all other purposes.

4. TOILETS

Status: Not implemented.
Description: Provision of individual toilets.
PO: Individual toilets will be built with UNICEF funds; these will consist of a double-pit latrine for each house.

CDC: There is a four-seat toilet block for women; men go to the beach. Some people have unsanitized latrines.

5. PRE-SCHOOL

Status: Not implemented.
Description: A local pre-school for the community children.

PO: The NHDA surveyed the community and selected the children. The school will start as soon as the community hall is completed, it will be furnished by UNICEF. Community members have agreed to pay Rs.5 a month for each child as teachers' wages.

CDC: Children are going to a nearby welfare pre-school (a quarter of a mile away). Community members have agreed to pay for local school.

6. HEALTH EDUCATION

Status: On-going.
Description: Lectures, support and immunization programmes.
PO: Immunizations, support for pregnant women and nutrition programmes have taken place already. A mobile clinic (as well as a mobile library) will be brought by the UC when the community hall is finished.

CDC: There is a welfare society clinic that takes care of the community's most immediate needs. A local clinic is desirable.

7. COMMUNITY HALL

Status: On-going.
Description: A physical place for meetings and other community-oriented activities such as child care, mobile clinics, etc. As of January 1987, a well-built community hall was in the final stage of construction.

PO: The hall was built with UNICEF assistance.

CDC: The UC has given small contracts to the Gramodaya Mandalaya (village council), which in turn hires local labour for the construction of the hall.

COMMENTS

The early construction of the community hall is beneficial by building confidence in the process, serving as a model or pattern for other construction and by providing the setting for community participation right from the beginning. One wonders whether efforts should be made in other communities to build a hall as if it were among the top priorities. Here the question is: to what extent can or should the workshops be influenced by previous experience?

8. SCHOOL DROP-OUTS

Status: Partially implemented.
Description: Training programmes and job opportunities for school drop-outs and young unemployed.

PO: Some jobs have been found around this furniture-making district. It is also a fishing district, and fishery-related jobs could be created. The PO and the UC have asked several governmental agencies to accept people into their training programmes; the UC has already surveyed the community.

CDC: There are 40 to 50 drop-outs in the community; no particular action has been taken except for a survey. Most drop-outs do have income-generating activities (repairing fishing nets, carpentry). A few have problems like alcoholism or gambling. Drugs are rare.

9. INCREASING INCOME

Status: No progress
Description: Organization and training for income-generating activities for the young, unemployed, and women, as a secondary source of income.

PO: There is an informal industrial assembly line throughout this furniture-making area. There are also the *Sramadanas* which have generated some income to the participants in two programmes: cleaning the site at the time of the blocking-out and road construction (prepare road-bed, cleaning boundaries, levelling, etc.).

CDC: The community has unsuccessfully requested UC assistance for the development of fishery and tools for carpentry. Some women join political organizations.

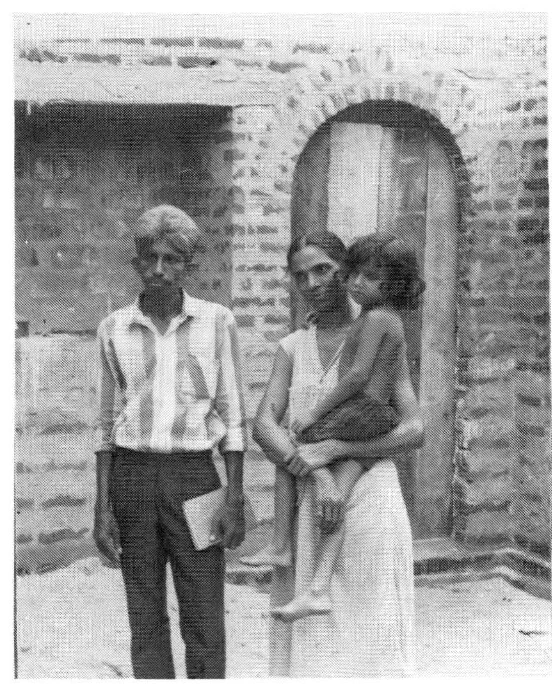

PROJECT: NUGAGAHAPURA

DATE OF WORKSHOP: 5–6 July 1986

UNITS: 54

FAMILIES: 64

This is a 30-year-old informal settlement within urban Columbo. It is well consolidated. The site was deeply excavated in the '40s and '50s to extract fill; it is up to 15m below its surroundings creating a very isolated and quiet environment. With one main entrance road and within steep slopes, it is a veritable cul-de-sac.

One of its main problems is that of land ownership. The land was acquired in 1956 by a Government Agent for the Labour Commissioner; it was neglected and soon squatted upon.

The local Municipal Council declared Nugagahapura a 'Low-income Housing Improvement Project Area,' a formal status that allows the NHDA to fund physical improvement. However, the NHDA has been unable to overcome the entangled bureaucracy of different agencies, and all its requests for land transferral have been unsuccessful. The land has not been regularized. CDC members have talked to the Mayor, the Government Agent and the NHDA, all to no avail.

Several CDC members were interviewed, including the chairman.

PRIORITIES/SOLUTIONS

1. Land ownership
(a) Inform relevant agencies
(b) Block-out land, get deeds
(c) Help identify boundaries, landmarks, etc.

2. Street lights
(a) Inform Electricity Board
(b) Help install posts

3. Permanent housing
Get loans

4. Drains
Repair and clean existing drains

5. Toilets
Repair existing toilets

6. Prematernal health
(a) Lectures, advice
(b) Direct to clinics

7. Unemployment
(a) Self-employment scheme for women: sewing, orchards
(b) Vocational youth training: technical, carpentry, masonry, electricity, etc.

8. Garbage dumping from surroundings
Take legal action

9. Mosquitoes and lice (stagnant water)
(a) Repair and clean drains
(b) Get the authority to lay and maintain main drains and pipes

10. Pathways (access to houses)
Fix during blocking-out

11. School drop-outs
Identify and direct to schools

12 Personal health
(a) Communication
(b) Posters, films
(c) Advice, lectures

13. Environmental health (garbage, drains, etc)
(a) Same as above
(b) voluntary works

14. Community hall
(a) Reserve land in blocking-out

(b) Build suitable community hall (Government funds, community labour)

15. Erosion of surrounding borders, earthslips
Seek immediate solution other than retaining walls (too expensive)

16. Drug addiction
(a) Same as 12, 13.
(b) Sports, leisure activities
(c) Employment after rehabilitation

17. Savings programme scheme
Organize systematic savings

18. Child nutrition
Get advice from health officers

19. Family health and planning
(a) Identify problems
(b) Get advice and instruction on methods

1. LAND OWNERSHIP

Status: Not implemented.
Description: Blocking-out of the land, getting deeds.

PO: No regularization has been possible.

CDC: The site has unclear boundaries due to past physical changes: excavations, landslides. There have been different surveys over the years. An exchange of correspondence has occurred. The community is willing to help with on-ground labour.

COMMENTS

Again, land ownership should be a priority, before anything else. It is a question of legal status and security of tenure as well as of self-confidence and dignity. Non-regularized squatters are non-taxpayers and thus neglected by the municipal council unless the NHDA constantly demands services. The community is willing to pay a very small, affordable tax of Rs.2 to Rs.15. The community cannot help itself much, though; it needs the support of an official organization or agency.

It would be better that land-ownership matters be managed at the municipal level; decisions here are taken at a much more centralized and inexpedient level.

Again one wonders whether land-tenure should be solved before attempting Microplanning workshops: the people are much less interested in the other issues (including health issues) when their main hope and starting point remains unfulfilled. In the words of the PO: 'The workshop is useful in identification of problems, but the community does not follow up. The CDC organizes *Sramadanas*, but not often enough. There are time limitations regarding the secondary priorities: most time is consumed in the main issue. If the regularization of tenure takes two and a half years, all the problems have to be explained again. Internal workshops could be held after the regularization.'

2. STREET LIGHTING

Status: Not implemented.
Description: Provision of appropriate lighting in public streets and paths.

PO: Street lights depend on blocking-out.

CDC: Same as PO.

3. PERMANENT HOUSING

Status: Not implemented.
Description: Mostly upgrading of existing houses; it is a comparatively well established community.

PO: This activity depends on blocking-out.

4. DRAINS

Status: Completed.
Description: Cleaning and repairing earth-drains.
PO: The officer thinks that the community completed this activity.

CDC: A *Sramadana* was held for the cleaning of drains. No repairs were needed because new drains were built only a year earlier by a Catholic NGO; the community does not want to build new drains until after the blocking-out because the layout may change, forcing them to undo whatever was built.

5. TOILETS

Status: Not implemented.
Description: Repairing of existing toilets.

PO: Very minor repairs have been done. 'The community doesn't know how to prioritize.' 'People won't implement improvements without land ownership first.'

CDC: The community repaired small defects. The CMC must empty the septic

tanks; it did once, but did not come back. In the words of a CDC member: 'The CMC isn't aware of Nugagahapura.'

6. PREMATERNAL HEALTH

Status: Implemented.
Description: Advice and support for pregnant women.

PO: This is the responsibility of the CMC's Area Health Warden. The PO does not know the extent of implementation: 'There's lack of communication between departments'; 'People have not complained: it must be all right.' If complaints were heard, the PO would directly turn to the agency involved.

CDC: The CMC Health Warden has brought a mobile clinic round twice in three months.

COMMENTS

As in previous cases, responsibilities are clearly delimited after the workshop. Most services must be taken care of by the CMC, while the NHDA (through the assigned PO) supervises the physical improvements and the administrative/bureaucratic framework behind them. This is indeed a heavy load for a single PO who must be in charge of several projects at the same time. It should not come as a surprise, then, that he is not aware of the progress of activities that he would much rather consider as outside his competence.

7. UNEMPLOYMENT

Status: On-going.
Description: Training for alternative income-generating activities.

PO: Not informed CDC/CMC's responsibility.

CDC: The CMC demonstrated the uses of the manioc flour at the request of the CDC. Also, US Save the Children is based nearby and has already trained six hospital attendants and has found them jobs; these people were identified and selected by the CDC. Only one family is generating additional income. Activities are varied; there are mainly workers and masons.

8. GARBAGE DUMPING FROM SURROUNDINGS

Status: On-going.
Description: Being an average of 10m below the surrounding neighbours, which are mainly earlier NHDA housing pro-

jects, and since they are informal squatters (in spite of their long permanence and development), this community is faced with the problem of having the neighbouring projects constantly dump their garbage onto their site.

PO: Not informed CDC/CMC's responsibility.

CDC: They still have a problem. The CMC helped them file their case in court against the neighbouring settlements which are generally better-off. The problem stopped for two to three months but has reappeared. 'CMC officials don't come around here much.' They have decided to write to the Chief Medical Officer of Health.

COMMENTS

One is inclined to wonder what makes the neighbouring communities dump their garbage onto this site, whether the garbage collection is simply inadequate or whether this community is being harrassed and despised probably because of its weak status or some other reason. It is also interesting to note that communities may need legal aid and advice. The authority should be well prepared to deal with legal issues such as land tenure, internal disputes requiring some kind of minor arbitrage or any legal circumstance in which the community may be involved.

Should a legal-aid Department exist? Should lawyers participate in the workshops?

9. MOSQUITOES AND LICE

Status: Not implemented.

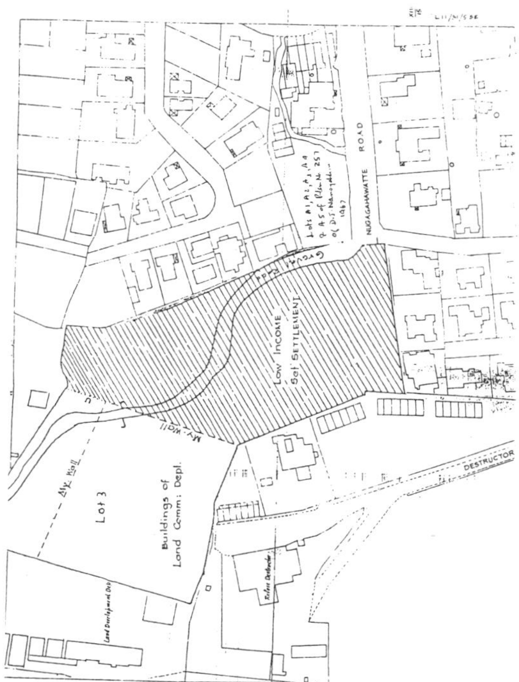

Description: Periodic spraying of insecticides, cleaning of garbage bins.

PO: Not informed. CDC/CMC's responsibility.

CDC: The community has cleaned the drains and keeps the garbage away from the doors. The CMC people do not come as often as needed. 'CMC workers come around and sell the insecticides instead of applying them.' denounces one community member. They have spoken to the CMC people but feel ignored. They wish to stop speaking to the CMC Health Wardens (who apparently cannot cope) and concentrate more on their housing issues.

10. INTERNAL ROADS, HOUSE ACCESS

Status: Not implemented.
Description: Building walkways from main road to the houses' entrances.

PO: This activity depends on blocking-out.

CDC: Same as PO.

11. SCHOOL DROP-OUTS

Status: On-going.
Description: Alternative activities and continuing education for young school drop-outs.

PO: Not informed.

CDC: A community-based 'children's society' has been created to organize activities and distribute books, clothes, stationery and other school-aid coming from different agencies.

12. PERSONAL HEALTH

Status: On-going.
Description: Consciousness-raising programme for personal hygiene.

PO: Not informed. CDC/CMC's responsibility.

CDC: There is a confusion between 'personal health' and 'disease-treatment' The CMC sent one film without giving a previous lecture or sending an accompanying person, which was felt to be insufficient by the community.

13. ENVIRONMENTAL HEALTH (GARBAGE)

Status: On-going.
Description: This priority deals mainly with the appropriate disposal of garbage.

PO: Not informed. CDC/CMC's responsibility.

CDC: A *Sramadana* was organized once after the workshop. The CMC sent a vehicle and the CDC loaded the garbage. The community now dumps garbage on site and occasionally burns it. The CMC gives plastic bags and collects them at the main entrance twice a week.

14. COMMUNITY HALL

Status: Not implemented.
Description: Construction of a community hall.

PO: This activity depends on the blocking-out, in which land will be allocated. Meanwhile, the community uses the open space it has always used, near the entrance.

CDC: Same as PO.

15. EROSION OF SURROUNDING BORDERS

Status: Not implemented.
Description: Because of the level difference, the site is surrounded by steep slopes that have eroded and partially collapsed. This becomes critical during the rainy seasons.

PO: The community has not had problems yet; it is not a priority activity.

CDC: Developers and owners of the surrounding areas have built retaining walls to protect their own properties, but many of these walls are old and are visibly breaking apart. Community members fear that these walls will collapse onto the houses at any time. The PO has requested NHDA engineers to survey and propose solutions.

COMMENTS

This seems to be a rather urgent problem with no apparent solution according to the available resources.

Moreover, it has fallen far below the first priorities and may not be taken care of for a long period of time.

This is the case of a priority that the community chose to downgrade in spite of its urgency, and one wonders whether the workshop should seek to give special attention to cases like this (that pose a threat to the community). As in the case of the construction of a community hall, the questions that arise here are: To what extent can criteria be forced through the workshop? How can the POs be more effective in presenting their case, in communicating the convenience or necessity of an action in view of their previous experience?

16. DRUG ADDICTION

Status: Implemented.
Description: Identification and rehabilitation of drug addicts.

PO: Not informed.

CDC: One family with drug problems was eventually thrown out of the community. There is no immediate problem.

17. SAVINGS PROGRAMME

Status: On-going.
Description: Organization of a Thrift and Credit Society as a preliminary step toward the offering of loans after the land-tenure is regularized.

PO: The first meeting of the local Thrift Society was held in December 1986. Monthly meetings have been organized, a board elected, a constitution prepared. At the third meeting, in January 1987, the collection of money started. There are plans of associating with a bank approved by the Co-operative Commissioner. Most of the 64 families will join the Society.

At the meetings the PO explained the importance and methods of saving; he helped the community to get together and organize; he attends all meetings and gives instructions for the following steps (how to go to the co-operative, prepare documents to get registered in the Co-operative Department as a Thrift and Credit Society, etc.) The whole process should last about half a year.

CDC: Preliminary discussions for a Thrift and Credit Society started in September. Already three or four general meetings have been held. A savings plan has just been initiated.

18. CHILD NUTRITION

Status: On-going.
Description: Treatments, care and educational programmes.

PO: Not informed.

CDC: There is a polyclinic nearby that takes care of the children once a month. Advice and some food were provided on-site once after the workshop by a NGO (US Save the Children). Also educational trips to town, parks and the zoo have been organized by the CDC.

19. FAMILY HEALTH AND PLANNING

Status: On-going.
Description: Treatments, care and educational programmes.

PO: Not informed.

CDC: The CMC has made available a clinic, advice and methods. There is a maternity hospital in which permanent sterilizations are practised.

PROJECT: SUMITHRARAMA

DATE OF WORKSHOP: 2–3 August, 1986

UNITS: 285

FAMILIES: 300

Sumithrarama is a rather large urban settlement developed mainly along a single road on a linear site, which was originally a fire gap belonging to the Colombo Municipal Council, CMC.

Involved agents are the NHDA, UNICEF and Redd-Barna, a Norwegian NGO committed to community and infrastructure development of this community. Redd-Barna identified this as a project area, built an on-site branch office and developed the first stages together with the Urban Development Authority.

Still belonging to the CMC, actual improvements were not allowed until NHDA's Deputy General Manager and Unit Manager succeeded in having the land transferred to them.

The size of this community posed organizational problems. At first political leaders were asked to organize the community but this would not work. For ease of management, the settlement was divided in three CDCs, one for every 100 families, each of which had a three-day workshop. Later one main council was formed, with a common fund of Rs.10 per capita, plus three sub-councils for subdivision purposes.

The blocking-out has been completed and most families were relocated within the same project area. For this purpose, additional land was acquired, although what was available was not enough: some 30 families had to be relocated elsewhere.

Besides speaking to several CDC members, it was possible to interview the on-site Redd-Barna officer, who has a full schedule five days a week at the branch office specially built for this purpose. He regularly attends CDC meetings. At the CMC District Office it was possible to talk to the Assistant Health Education Officer — who pays weekly visits to the settlement, attends CDC meetings and keeps in touch with the NHDA's PO — and to the District Engineer, who was not familiar with the workshop or its outcome.

PRIORITIES/SOLUTIONS

1. Housing
Programme savings plan

2. Garbage
Inform relevant authorities

3. Toilets
Renovate

4. Unemployment
Promote self-employment

5. Potable water
Repair taps (Government)

6. Ownership of land
Regularize ownership of building blocks

7. Electricity
Repair electric wires and cables

8. Postal services
Assign numbers to houses (Government)

9. Drugs
Lectures, films and discussions

10. Health advice to mothers
Advise and direct to health centres

11. Food stamps
Request from authority

12. Community centre
Allocate adequate land in blocking-out

13. Drain
Repair and renovate

14. Malnutrition
Inform health educational centres and institutions

15. Environmental pollution
Discuss with relevant institutions

16. Pre-school
Get aid and funding to improve and strengthen

17. Floods
Build temporary earth drain

1. HOUSING

Status: On-going.
Description: Upgrading of dwellings.

PO: Blocking-out completed; NHDA has made available loans of Rs.15,000 and technical assistance for self-help construction.

CDC: The change of the PO in the middle of the process caused a great delay (of about six months). A bank account was opened with the participation of 75 per cent of the community. 'Our main issues are housing, immunizations and maintenance of toilets,' says one member (Priorities 1–6, 10, 3).

COMMENTS

Delays were due to the transferral of the former PO, who was overloaded with work (handling seven similar projects at the same time) and with the aggravation of inadequate transport. After discussing with her superiors (that is, the Deputy General Manager and the Unit Manager), she was able to turn over five projects, including this one, to other POs.

Another cause of delay in this case is that all surveys of the site were done by private surveyors, selected and hired by the NGO since it was funding the blocking-out. Selection procedures were very slow, and the PO complained personally.

2. GARBAGE

Status: On-going.
Description: Appropriate disposal and collection of garbage.

PO: The garbage is not collected regularly. As people do not pay taxes because of their unofficial status, they are neglected by the CMC, which is responsible for this task. The PO helps organize community meetings as often as necessary or at least twice a month.

CDC: The CMC comes twice a week, which is not enough. The community

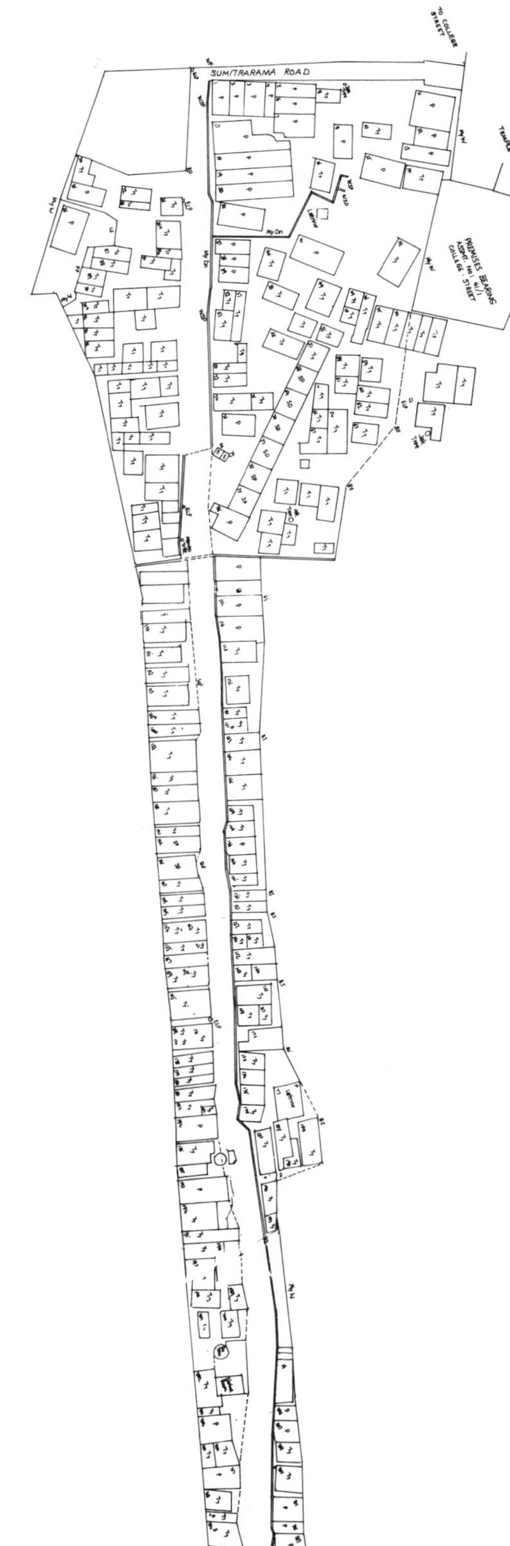

feels neglected because they are not tax-payers. Sometimes the influence of a Health Warden or a visiting Minister is useful.

CMC Health Warden: The CMC distributes free plastic garbage bags twice a week, but these are not used.

CMC District Engineer: Garbage is collected daily. Concrete garbage bins have been erected by CMC workers; garbage bags are distributed through the CDC to be collected between 9.30 and 12.00 a.m. but they are not used. The District has three tractors and five containers for the collection of garbage. 'We lack co-operation,' complains the Engineer.

COMMENTS

Perhaps garbage is not collected daily, but on the other hand the community has not complied with the simple requirement of using the plastic bags which would speed the collection process and improve environmental health. Plagued by flies and crows, garbage is dumped in bins right off the main street, from where it is shovelled into the CMC container brought by a tractor. The operation of emptying a bin lasts about ten minutes, during which two operators take turns at shovelling. The container is relatively small and one would expect that it must be emptied several times a day. Collecting bags would not only be faster and healthier but it would allow the use of other vehicles (open trucks, trailers, etc.). The bags are used for other purposes and their benefit is not understood. The use of plastic bags would certainly improve the environmental conditions of the community; however, it is worth noting that plastic is also a form of pollution, and in this case even its cost (of producing or importing it) may be worth taking into consideration. Perhaps the solution lies eleswhere.

3. TOILETS

Status: On-going.
Description: Construction of new toilet blocks.

PO: The NHDA and the CDC chose new sites for toilet blocks after the blocking-out; the NGO builds the toilets with community labour. Existing toilets were repaired as a temporary solution, but they will eventually be demolished.

CDC: The land was allocated. The CDC requested from the NGO a toilet-block for men.

Redd-Barna officer: A complete project and budget of Rs.50,000 for a toilet block were presented after the blocking-out; money and technical advice were given to this community-managed process in which people had the choice of volunteering or contracting labour. Whatever savings on the budget would go to a fund to be used for maintenance or other purposes.

4. UNEMPLOYMENT

Status: On-going.
Description: Programmes for alternative income-generating activities.

PO: The NHDA and UNICEF surveyed the women. After selecting 10 to 15 women, NHDA will make available loans to the CDC, which in turn will lend small amounts to these women so as to stimulate income-generating activities. Loans are of Rs.1,000 maximum, with Rs.25 to Rs.50 repayment monthly instalments.

CDC: Not informed.

Redd-Barna officer: A sewing teacher was paid for by the community collecting Rs.10 a month from each student. If successful, the NGO would eventually cover those wages.

5. POTABLE WATER

Status: Not implemented.
Description: Maintenance of water taps, provision of new outlets.
PO: Water taps were repaired by the NGO at the same time as the toilets. Location for future water taps is already determined; toilets are priority locations. There will be no new temporary taps.

CDC: Same as PO.

6. OWNERSHIP OF LAND

Status: On-going.
Description: Blocking-out and getting deeds.

PO: The blocking-out is complete. Deeds will be given, after the upgrading of houses and infrastructure, in a public opening ceremony. Some areas belonging to other government agencies have not yet been transferred to the NHDA. The PO has sent out reminders to the Land Officer without reply.

CDC: The land has been demarcated and Rs.15,000 loans are expected after the blocking-out is completed (that is, after each family is relocated).

Redd-Barna officer: The NGO did the land surveys following NHDA directions; as the surveyors are under contract the process is faster than if done by the NHDA's Survey Branch, which is 'slow, inefficient, poor.' The NHDA demarcated the land. Both NGO and NHDA officers get together regularly on-site and keep each other informed.

7. ELECTRICITY

Status: Not implemented.
Description: Repairs of existing cables; eventually underground installation.

PO: The Electriticity Board did minor repairs.

CDC: The damaged cables remain unrepaired. One month after the workshop, the CDC wrote to the CMC without reply.

8. POSTAL SERVICES

Status: Not implemented.
Description: Assignment of numbers for individualization and identification of houses so as to receive postal service.

PO: All lots have not been allocated yet. The NHDA will send a list to the CMC which will in turn assign the numbers.

CDC: Same as PO.

9. DRUGS

Status: Not implemented.
Description: Identification and rehabilitation of drug addicts.

PO: The CMC should conduct a survey with the help of the CDC.

CDC: The CDC informed the authorities of five heroin addicts and some alcoholism problems. The exposure resulted in arrests and fines, but the police raids are usually ineffective. No films or lectures on drugs have been brought to the site.

CMC Health Warden: There is an annual implementation plan at district level, 'but there's lack of participation; they believe this problem unimportant.' Lectures were given, some leaders trained, and posters were done on the initiative of the CMC by the community's children. A door-to-door survey was carried out.

COMMENTS

Often there are discrepancies between the CDC and the CMC versions that are hard to understand. One is bound to think that the entire community could not be fully aware of every activity that takes place; on the othe hand, a CMC officer may not be willing to accept evidence of negligence or delay regarding certain matters when interviewed by an outsider. Without attempting to make any judgement, this comment aims at acknowledging such discrepancies.

10. HEALTH ADVICE TO MOTHERS

Status: On-going.
Description: Advice to pregnant women and mothers.

PO: The CMC has a nutrition and polio immunization programme on-going.

CDC: There has been an immunization programme, films, and lectures by the Health Warden of the CMC.

CMC Health Warden: There was a programme ('Little Mother Class') with lectures once a week for three months. 'But housing is a burning issue,' says the HW, 'and until it is solved the community does not care much for health issues.'

11. FOOD STAMPS

Status: On-going.
Description: Selection of the community members that qualify to receive food stamps.

PO: The NHDA assisted the CDC to survey the community and identify the beneficiaries for food stamps to later inform the NGO.

CDC: The CDC and the PO informed the Food Department after the recipients were identified.

12. COMMUNITY CENTRE

Status: On-going.
Description: Construction of a hall for common events.

PO: The land was allocated at the blocking-out. The CDC and the NGO should now decide how to fund, what to build and how to build.

CDC: Two lots were requested from the NHDA. The halls will be funded by Redd-Barna, the NGO.

13. DRAINAGE

Status: Not implemented.
Description: Maintenance and construction of permanent drains.

PO: The CMC cleaned the existing drains once. New drains will not be built until completion of the blocking-out.

CDC: Internal conflicts within the CDC (between the president and the rest of the committee) and a lapse in the blocking-out stopped all progress on these works.

CMC District Engineer: The drains have been maintained; only a temporary solution is available. New drains are to be built by the NHDA, for which eight labourers have been assigned.

COMMENTS

According to members of the community, the president or chairman of the CDC is an old partisan who gets 'political favours' from the local minister or other authorities. It was argued that he got a larger lot with better access in the blocking-out, which was done by private surveyors hired by the NGO. This led to a sharp conflict between the community and their president. There also seems to be disagreement between the CDC president and the community regarding the general use of the land. A general meeting has been arranged to see whether the president is still representative of the community or not. This is an example of an internal affair that affects the process and about which the PO has little or nothing to do. He can only provide the means for the community to solve its problems internally. In this particular case, the PO seemed to keep a reasonable distance from the events although he supported the community members.

14. MALNUTRITION

Status: On-going.
Description: Treatment, care and education.

PO: The PO informed the CMC.

CDC: The CMC's Health Warden did an initial survey, identifying problems in the community, and then two nurses carried out a door-to-door survey and offered treatment and medicines. The CMC has provided continuous treatment for most cases in a clinic located half a mile away, three times a week for children and twice a week for pregnant women and mothers. There were films and lectures offered twice one month after the workshop.

CMC Health Warden: The CMC keeps a Growth Monitoring Chart for the children. Periodic meetings in which children are weighed are held at a neighbouring temple. The children's programme was not completed last year because there was a priority immunization programme taking place at the metropolitan level. 'It is important to create awareness before implementing. If you advertise a meeting on housing, they all attend; if it's health issues, many less come.'

15. ENVIRONMENTAL POLLUTION

Status: Not implemented.
Description: Prevention of pollution.

PO: The NHDA must insist that certain things be done, such as cleaning the septic tanks, collecting garbage, protesting and preventing the neighbouring tobacco factory from polluting the water in the surrounding canal. The PO thinks that he and the CDC members should go together to speak to the CMC, 'but to the people these are matters of a lesser priority and get delayed.'

CDC: The tobacco factory has solved the problem of water pollution.

16. PRE-SCHOOL

Status: On-going.
Description: Facilities and teachers for a pre-school.

PO: A school was furnished by UNICEF; teachers are temporarily being paid by Redd-Barna, but this arrangement will not last long. The community is thinking of ways to raise funds for the future wages.

CDC: The school is going on successfully managed by the CDC with 45 to 50 children. The CDC pays the teachers for their bus fares with money collected from throughout the community. Currently, the teachers are working without pay as volunteers, while the CDC requests Rs.500 from Redd-Barna.

17. FLOODS

Status: Not implemented.
Description: Construction programme of drains.

PO: A programme of construction of permanent drains will be carried out after the blocking-out. Temporary drains as a permanent solution are described in No. 13.

CDC: The problem is that there is an outlet in one of the boundary walls through which the collected waters pour into a major stream. This opening is too small to enable the water through, flooding the lower area of the settlement. All actions have been delayed until after the blocking-out, and not even temporary solutions have been attempted.

COMMENTS

Although some temporary solutions appeared very simple to carry out, the community members interviewed were reluctant to do 'things that will have to

be done again,' in spite of the small effort involved and the evident benefit. It is worth noting that, as one among the best supported communities, it lacks what could be defined as 'punch,' perhaps due to its size, perhaps due to the rather generous support it gets from several organizations. This is difficult to judge and measure, but perhaps the workshop lacked definition regarding certain activities or responsibilities, or that the community lost momentum as time passed and energies were spent in trying to solve top priorities. It may also be a question of both. It is also worth noting that in Sumithrarama the workshop resulted in a more elaborate and longer list of priorities than usual, and one suspects that the community cannot keep track of the entire process and of the relationships of the different priorities with improvements. In other words (as has been said before): main issues and secondary issues should be differentiated both during the workshop and implementation stage in terms of meaning, allocation of time and resources, feasibility, etc. A means of keeping track of the process of implementation should be devised in such a way that the community can recognize where it stands and what it can expect.

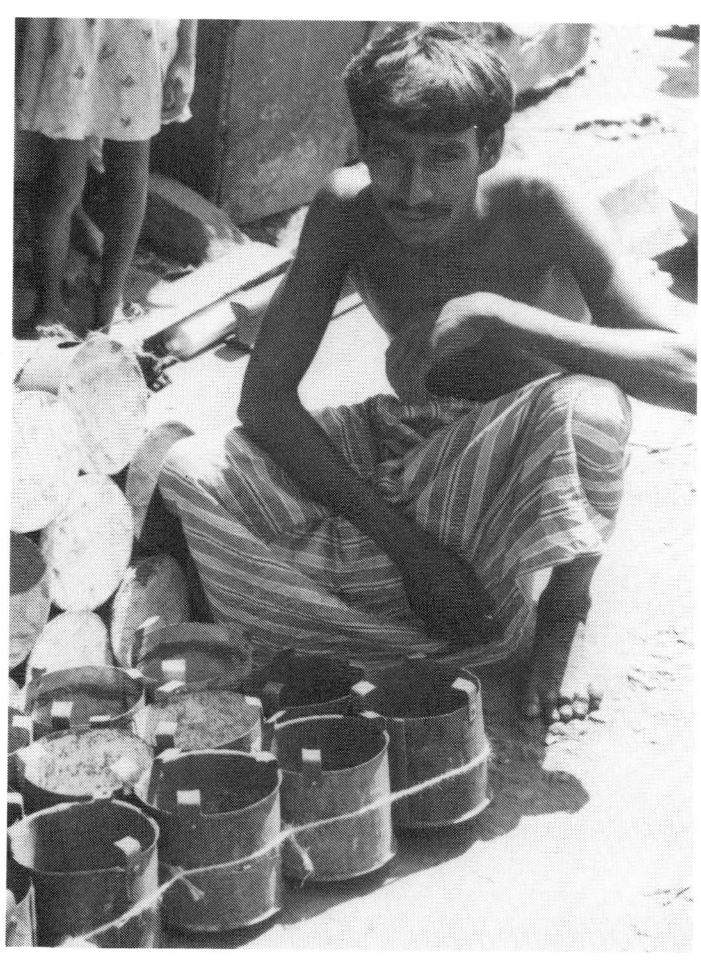

RECOMMENDATIONS

This final section is intended to consolidate the main observations and conclusions. They are presented in the form of proposals for specific action that can be added to the current procedures of the Microplanning workshop, or as topics that should be included in the workshop discussion.

ON THE PROCESS

1. UNDERSTAND THE DILEMMA: Top priorities are often the hardest, slowest and most expensive to implement; this must be understood in order to avoid frustration and loss of momentum.

2. CONSIDER BASIC ACTIONS PRIOR TO THE WORKSHOP: Land tenure, blocking-out and major physical improvements are usually top priorities that demand great effort and take so long to implement that all other priorities are underestimated and even forgotten about. Since these are found in almost all cases and often these are necessarily to most other priorities, these actions may well take place out of the context of the Microplanning workshop.

ON THE WORKSHOP

3. MODULATE WORKSHOP: Allocate more time for some (more complex, expensive) priorities and less for others, or:

4. BREAK DOWN WORKSHOP: Consider dividing the workshop into different sessions or even stages according to progress (Stage 1: top priorities; when almost completed, Stage 2: secondary priorities).

5. INFLUENCE THE WORKSHOP: Encourage some priorities as a result of previous experiences and to the benefit of the process; for instance: build a community hall first, or encourage technical assistance, use of loans, safety, environmental and other health-related issues, etc. This is essentially a matter of skill in communication by the project officers; they must learn how to present their cases convincingly.

6. ESTABLISH A CRITICAL PATH OF ACTIVITIES: An implementation diagram would be of great assistance in avoiding conflicting activities, unexpected delays, and to discover possible short cuts and time margins. This normally could be done by the project officers after the workshop, but it may be considered as part of the workshop itself.

7. BREAK DOWN SOLUTIONS IN STAGES: This renders them more feasible and may achieve early progress. This phrasing could be worked out in a PERT-type diagram and should be clearly understood by the community.

8. ESTABLISH PROPORTIONAL TASKS: These should be established according to the possibilities and potentials of the community in terms of scale, time, resources, skills. The *Sramadana* may not be effective for large-scale operations such as earth-filling of the entire settlement but appropriate for building a toilet block.

9. PROVIDE LEGAL AID/COUNSEL: This would be particularly useful at the time of the workshop and during the implementation period. It may be possible to create such a service at the NHDA, for often the major issues or priorities involve significant legal action.

ON THE IMPLEMENTATION STAGE

10. PROVIDE PERIODIC INFORMATION ON THE PROGRESS: This could be in the form of some graphic device which allows the community to understand easily, at any point or time, the state of achievement, reasons for delays and other characteristics of the process.

11. PROVIDE A TEMPORARY LEGAL STATUS: This ensures due recognition by administrative entities (CMC and the question of prompt garbage collection, for instance) and neighbours; which encourages participation, involvement, commitment and momentum.

12. RELIEVE THE POs/REINFORCE THE CDCs IN THE MANAGEMENT OF THE IMPLEMENTATION PROCESS: This gives more authority and control to the CDC by way of explicit recognition at the CMC level. Create a *logbook* or similar instrument in which the different stages and events of the implementation process be recorded so as to minimize dependence of the community on individual POs. This document could describe the evolution of each priority (visits, exchange of mail, problems, etc.) in a way that could be useful for systematic and broader evaluation purposes.

13. DECENTRALIZE DECISION-MAKING/REINFORCE THE CMCs IN THE LOCAL MANAGEMENT: Encourage more decisions to be taken at the local (municipal) level; particularly in matters regarding land tenure and boundaries.

14. HAVE STANDARD PROCEDURES BETWEEN AGENCIES: Communications, payments, contracts, transferrals, division of responsibilities, etc., should all be clarified and understood.

15. SUPPORT NEWCOMERS/OUTSIDERS AND MINORITIES: Provide special counselling (a morning session, for instance), the better to integrate this group.

SECTION II

THE HANDBOOK

This section contains the Microplanning Handbook in full. It is included in order that the reader may conduct his own Microplanning workshop sessions.

DEFINITIONS

Workshop Leader
- the leader, moderator, or "mediator" of the workshop.

Facilitators
- additional helpers, either brought along by the Workshop Leader or selected and oriented at the workshop.

Participants
- the individual participants of the workshop; they provide the basic resource for the workshop.

Group
- the term used to identify the different representatives: health and social development group, community group, technical (architect, engineer, planner) group.

Team
- the term used to identify the participants when two or more groups are combined to jointly address issues

Stages - (prepared *FOR THE WORKSHOP LEADER*) the broad task area.

Steps
- (prepared *FOR THE PARTICIPANTS*) the actions within each stage in order to carry out the broad task

Tasks
- things you have to do to acomplish your objectives

Chart
- a summary table prepared on a large sheet of paper and intended to be pinned or taped on the wall.

Guidebook Format
- *Descriptions for Workshop Leader:* Plain text.
- *Steps for Participants:* Text setoff by lined box.
- *Examples from previous work:* Handwritten text or drawings

CONTENTS

INTRODUCTION AND METHOD

One of the critical questions facing the urban sub-program of the National Housing Development Authority remains: How to expand the scale of housing programs to satisfy the unprecedented demand for both new and improved housing.

In response, three related general trends are distinguishable within NHDA housing policy:
First, the shift away from government dominated supply, and toward locally initiated and implementable programs.
Second, the emphasis on fast, participatory, action-based planning and implementation, relying less on strategic planning, and more on immediate needs.
Third, the emphasis on skills training largely directed at building a cadre of technical and managerial personnel who can work locally with government and non-government organizations.

These trends have evolved during the past four years, but they are not new to development theorists nor to housing practitioners. The question however, is how to translate theory into sound practice, in such a way to avoid overly technical systems or untried models (both causes for past failures).

This handbook describes a process for doing just that: an "Action Planning" procedure, not so much intended to "tell what to do", but rather, to describe "how to find out what to do" (program making) and then, "how to go about doing it" (implementation). It fits within the broader and innovative housing program of Sri Lanka, with its 'support' rather than 'supply' policies.

The handbook provides local personnel with tools which enables plans to be developed (for example for a neighborhood of 20 families) within a few days. It is intensely participatory and action based. The minimum amount of information is collected in order to inform decision making, and long surveys, and sophisticated data management, are all avoided. The implementation team is assumed to include residents, technical personnel and health and social workers.

Its methods (rather than systems or models) introduce quick, easy techniques for program making, design, implementation and monitoring. These are structured to balance the need for strategic planning with local more spontaneous action: problem seeking with problem solving; community needs, with government objectives; off-site preparation with on-site development and implementation. Training is designed to go hand-in-hand with implementation, following "learning by doing" principles, and then helping to accelerate development. The handbook is structured to provide a general and therefore non-context specific framework, which is locally interpretable, to reflect local issues and needs.

In summary there are two broad objectives:
1. To act as a **FIELD HANDBOOK** for community groups and technical and professional staff, guiding the various phases of project development, from program-making through to implementation and monitoring.
2. To **TRAIN TECHNICAL AND MANAGEMENT STAFF** to work locally, in a manner which is participatory, community based and 'action' oriented.

The handbook includes 5 related but autonomous parts, which can be used singly or together, depending on local circumstances. Their order, as presented here, is not intended to direct project sequencing - only to reflect convention. The parts are:

1. Identification: What are the Problems?
2. Strategies: What are the Approaches?
3. Options and Tradeoffs: What are the Actions?
4. Planning for Implementation: Who does What When and How?
5. Monitoring: What is the Performance and What have we Learned?

SUMMARY

STAGE I

Identification
WHAT ARE THE PROBLEMS?

• STEP 1:
MAKE FIELD SURVEY

• STEP 2:
PREPARE LIST OF PROBLEMS

Problem	Why?	To Whom ?

• STEP 3:
AGREE ON PROBLEMS

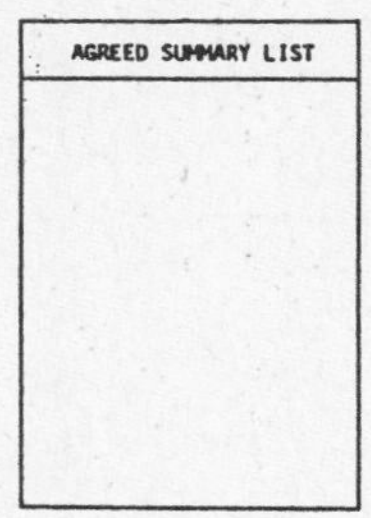

• STEP 4:
CONSIDER HEALTH ISSUES

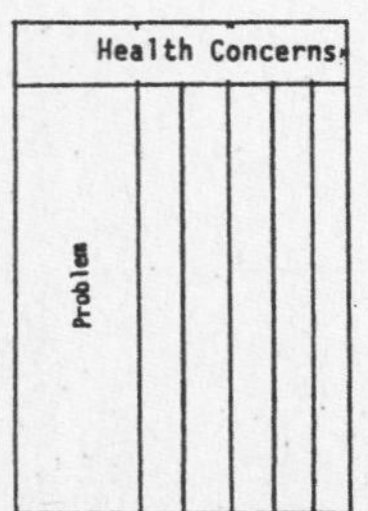

STAGE II

Strategies
WHAT ARE THE APPROACHES?

• STEP 1:
LIST STRATEGIES

Problem	Immediate Action	Long-Term Action
(List all agreed problems)		

• STEP 2:
MAKE PRIORITIES

	ALL AGREE	2 teams agree	1 team only
1st priority			
2nd priority			
3rd priority			

• STEP 3:
AGREE ON PRIORITIES

AGREED SUMMARY LIST	
Problem	Action

STAGE III

Options and tradeoffs
WHAT ARE THE ACTIONS?

- **STEP 1:**
LIST OPTIONS

EACH ACTION		
Options	G	G+C
1.		
2.		
3.		
4.		

- **STEP 2:**
NEGOTIATE AND SELECT OPTIONS

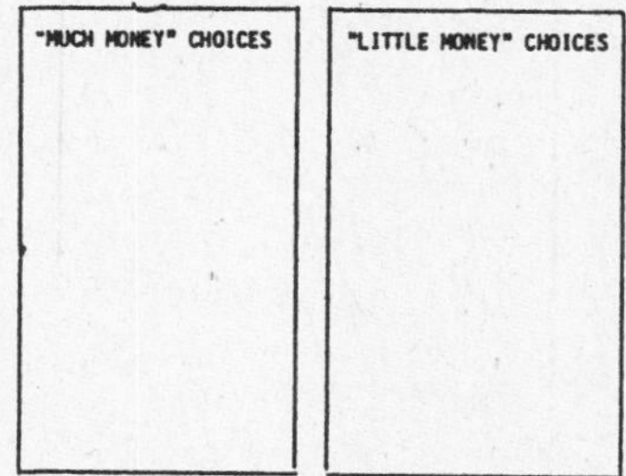

STAGE IV

Planning for implementation
WHO DOES WHAT WHEN AND HOW?

- **STEP 1:**
LIST TASKS

EACH OPTION CHOSEN		
Tasks	Who	What and How
1.		
2.		
3.		
4.		

- **STEP 2A:**
LOCATE PLANNED SITE IMPROVEMENTS

Site Plan :

Location criteria :

- **STEP 2B:**
IDENTIFY NEEDED HOUSE IMPROVEMENTS

Plan :

Section :

Recommendations :

STAGE V

Monitoring
HOW IS IT WORKING?
AND WHAT CAN WE LEARN?

- **STEP 1:**
DESCRIBE THE SITUATION

Status	How is It Working?	Who Maintains It?

- **STEP 2:**
DRAW LESSONS FROM EXPERIENCE

Status	What To Be Done To CORRECT Next Time	What To Be Done To AVOID Next Time

GETTING STARTED

WHAT STAFF IS REQUIRED?

• A *Workshop Leader*, a *Logistics Officer* who takes care of all of the arrangements, and a *Project Officer* form the core team for running the workshop. These three are responsible for the success of the workshop. In addition, several "helpers" are often useful to pin up charts, move tables, etc., during the sessions.

• The *WORKSHOP LEADER* (or teacher) may be drawn from the university staff. He is in overall charge of the workshop.

• The *LOGISTICS OFFICER* is either from the central or local authority. He provides the link with overall policy and provides training materials as needed.

• The *PROJECT OFFICER* is from the local authority. He represents the on-site support, and is responsible for seeing that the work is carried out after the work program (the "Micro-Plan") is prepared at the end of the Workshop.

• The *FACILITATORS* are the key "non-visible" members. Three are needed and should be selected by the Workshop Leader, perhaps from the participants themselves. One will sit with each of the three groups to be formed in the workshop: one to work with technical group, one with health and social development group, and one with community group. The Facilitator cannot be the spokesman for the groups. He can only help the groups to express themselves, particularly with the community groups to overcome shyness! (It may be helpful for the Workshop Leader to meet with the Facilitators each day to review the steps.)

• Several *TECHNICAL PERSONNEL* will be needed to review the technical needs of the community.

• Several *HEALTH AND SOCIAL DEVELOPMENT PERSONNEL* will be needed to review the health and social needs of the community.

• And most important, the *COMMUNITY REPRESENTATIVES!* Approximately 8-12 people should be selected to represent all of the community. How are these representatives selected? The following is a guide:
- Select the present leader of the Community Development Council

(Chairman and Secretary perhaps).
- Select approximately 8 people who are a good cross-section of age (younger members and very senior members), ethnic groups (one from each), and sex (there should be at least two ladies as representatives).
- Select any others who people in the community identified as active in events of the community.

WHO IS RESPONSIBLE?

• The three core organizers must decide among themselves how to divide the tasks in preparation and conduct of the Workshop. They should meet well before the planned dates of the Workshop and talk this over. The following is a general list of things to do:

Task	*Workshop Leader*	*Logistics Officer*	*Project Officer*
Organize organizers			
Conduct initial community meetings			
Lead overall workshop			
Coordinate central authority support			
Arrange on-site logistics			
Select community group			
Select technical group			
Select social group			
Explain workshop stages			
Organize workshop stages			
Document workshop			
Follow-up on agreements			

WHAT DO WE HAVE TO ARRANGE?

Meet with the Community:

• Get together with the community before the workshop to explain objectives and the program of the workshops. It may be useful to have summary charts of the program and the objectives and post them at the community before hand. How can we make the community more aware of the objectives and the program?
1) Put up summary charts of the program beforehand in the community meeting place or other public place.
2) Pass out pamphlets which explain what the goals are.

• In the meetings, make sure that the community is clear about the purpose of the workshop: "they will prepare a work program which will commit the authorities and the community to joint improvement efforts".

- Assure a representative selection from the CDC's of the community
- Make sure that there is a strong commitment by the community in the efforts. Equally, explain that the NHDA and UNICEF are strongly committed to supporting the community's efforts in improving the neighborhood. Make clear that not everything can be done at once, or that everything that is needed can be provided.

Decide where to meet:

- Determine where the workshop location will be; be sure to inspect the place before you start: avoid last minute surprises!
- Assure that sufficient wall space is available to pin-up or hang the charts.

Get necessary materials:

- Flip chart with sufficient paper for charts
- Program worksheets which explain who does what on a day-by-day basis
- Markers, different colours; have on hand a minimum of five
- Tape or pins to attach charts to wall
- Sufficient tables and chairs for participants
- Base plan of area to be dealt with, or make a base plan.
- Folder for each participant, which includes: paper, pencil, schedule, base plan of area
- Polaroid camera (optional)
- A bell or whistle to call the meetings to order!

Arrange for food:

- Arrange for lunches for all of the participants for the two days
- Arrange for tea, cups, etc. for the two tea breaks each day; and make clear at what times tea will be served; the ladies of the communities may be helpful with this!

HOW DO WE CONDUCT THE SESSION?

- Participants should be led to discover for themselves, both ideas and options. These should not be prescribed by the instructor.
- Participants should be encouraged to perceive problems, issues and solutions through the eyes of the various actors with whom they will have to deal when undertaking their job. Role playing is a useful technique in this respect. Remember that the participants are familiar with the problems, just that the setting is different.
- Local people often have a better understanding of local issues than experts from the outside, who may come from differing locations or countries.
- Each session should start with a summary of the previous day's activities and with an outline of what is to come.
- Each day should end with summary of the day's activities listed on a flip chart or equivalent. The old adage applies here:

  tell them what you're going to tell them (or do)
  tell it to them (or do it)
  tell them what you told them (or what you did)

- Adhere to schedules promptly, but with adequate flexibility to incorporate ideas, which may be pertinent, or to spend additional time where it may be beneficial.
- Keep breaks (lunch, tea, etc.) short. It is better to finish the day early than to extend breaks, or to fill in time.
- During discussions or participant responses, ensure that only one discussion is being conducted at any one time.
- Throughout discussions illustrate issues and points with concrete examples which participants can identify with. Minimize abstract diagrams or ideas.
- Summarize what you have said several times to make sure people have understood. Repeat entire sessions through on the spot "mini-exercises" if needed to clarify issues.
- Control wandering during presentations!
- Point to charts when you talk about them; place charts to be visible.
- Go around and see how people are getting on during the work. Remind people of what they're doing!

- The following table may be useful in planning the workshop. For each activity planned, five things should be considered:

time (when start, when end; how long)
activity (what is planned to do)
topics (what will be covered)
team arrangement (how the groups will be seated)
comments (things you should keep in mind)

The following is an example of a schedule table:

Indicative Time	Activity	Topic	Team Arrangement	Comments
11.00-12.15	PREPARE LIST OF PROBLEMS - Teams prepare chart and present to group CHART ①	Chart includes 1) Problem 2) Why it is a problem 3) To whom it is a problem Workshop leaders should go through detailed example Limit problems to 1 sheet of paper	- Same 3 teams grouped around separate tables - Spokesman selected by each team - Facilitator should assist in grouping problem areas.	- 3 charts are prepared, one from each team - Ask teams how they found out it was a problem - Discuss what is not agreed, why do some see it as a problem, others not, and what criteria was used in deciding.
12.15-1.00	AGREE ON PROBLEMS - Prepare summary chart of problem areas, by Workshop Leaders CHART ②	- List all problems and indicate team who viewed it as a problem - If problem only appears once, team must convince other 2 teams to accept.		- If problem selected by two teams, it is accepted - Consider using a voting situation to select problems: each team one vote.
	- Prepare matrix of all problems, by workshop leaders	- List all problems along both horizontal and vertical sides - Selected health official discusses linkages to health and child care - Use solid dots if strong linkage, hollow dot if weak linkage		- Purpose is to develop awareness of health issues and their relation to basic physical problems - This activity may be delayed until after lunch
1.00 - 2.00	LUNCH			

The following table can be used by you to fill out:

Indicative Time	Activity	Topic	Team Arrangement	Comments

THE OPENING SESSION

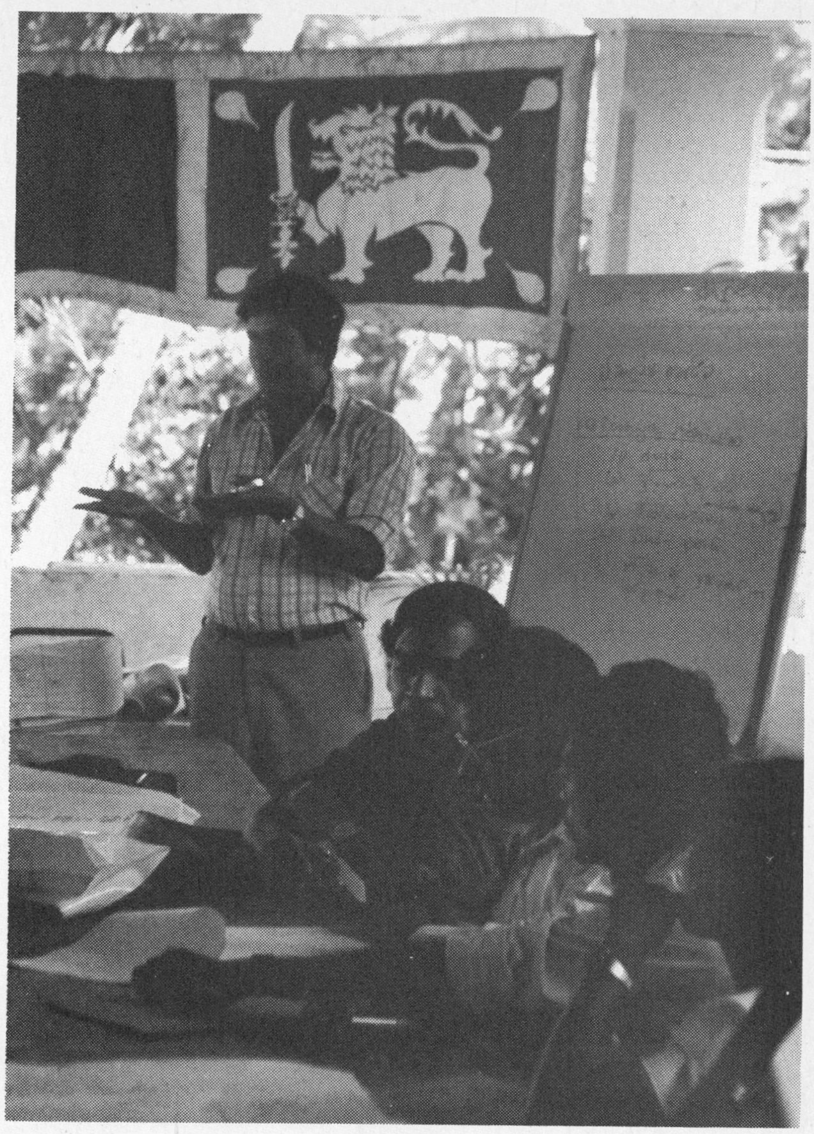

WHAT IS THE TASK?

The first meeting with all of the groups is the most important. Several things should be accomplished:

- Make clear the **PURPOSE** so everyone understands the key objectives and the outcome at the end of the workshop. Stress that the main goal is to produce an upgrading plan for the neighborhood.

- Make clear the **CONTEXT** of the training program. Answer the question: "How does this program fit with the government policies of the Million Houses Program?" It may be useful to *briefly* review the Million Houses Program.

- Make clear the **PROGRAM** for the next days. Explain in detail what will happen each session. Hand out a schedule to each person so he can follow you as you explaiin.

- Make clear the **PROCEDURE** to be followed in the stages. Explain that they will be "role-playing," and what this means. Stress that they will be actively participating in all of the sessions, through preparing charts, interviewing and surveying families and communities, and group discussions.

- And most important, **ESTABLISH A RAPPORT** with the participants! Get them interested and enthusiastic in what they will do.

HOW DO GO ABOUT DOING IT?

The workshop should be formally opened with a joint statement by the community leader and an NHDA official. The workshop leader will be introduced, who will then direct the sessions.

Each of the different groups will be called on to give a brief opening statement: a technical group representative and a health and social development group representative. They will discuss what their *role* is, and briefly outline their *key concerns.*

WHAT IS THE OUTCOME?

All should have a clear idea of the purpose and the schedule, and know who the people are.

HOW DO WE SIT?

No specific seating is needed. All sit intermixed. Other community members may participate, but the official community representives should be clearly identified.

WHAT MATERIALS AND EQUIPMENT DO WE NEED?

Only a summary chart of the schedule and stages is needed. Tape or pin this on the wall so it can be seen by all.

THINGS TO CONSIDER

- Stress throughout that the workshop will be dealing with real problems and the goal is to develop real solutions.

- Keep the opening introductions very short. They are just introductions, nothing more.

- The symbolic nature of the opening is very important. A high official of the NHDA is needed to show the seriousness of the commitment.

[illegible]

GENERAL OBJECTIVES

(1) TO IMPROVE PHYSICAL CONDITIONS AND BASIC SERVICES IN EACH URBAN CENTRE

[illegible]

(2) TO LINK SOCIAL PLANNING + SERVICES FOR CHILDREN WITH PHYSICAL + SOCIAL IMPROVEMENTS.

[illegible]

(3) TO FOCUS INTERVENTIONS SPECIFICALLY TO IMPROVE CHILD SURVIVAL + DEVELOPMENT

[illegible]

[illegible]

WORKSHOP OBJECTIVES

(1) TO TRAIN TRAINORS IN NEEDS ASSESSMENT & MAKING MICRO PLANS, QUICKLY AND EFFECTIVELY.

[illegible]

(2) TO MAKE MICRO PLANS TO IMPROVE THIS NEIGHBOURHOOD

[illegible]

(3) TO MOBILISE COMMUNITY ACTION IN PREPARATION FOR THE IMPLEMENTATION OF IMPROVEMENT PLANS

[illegible]

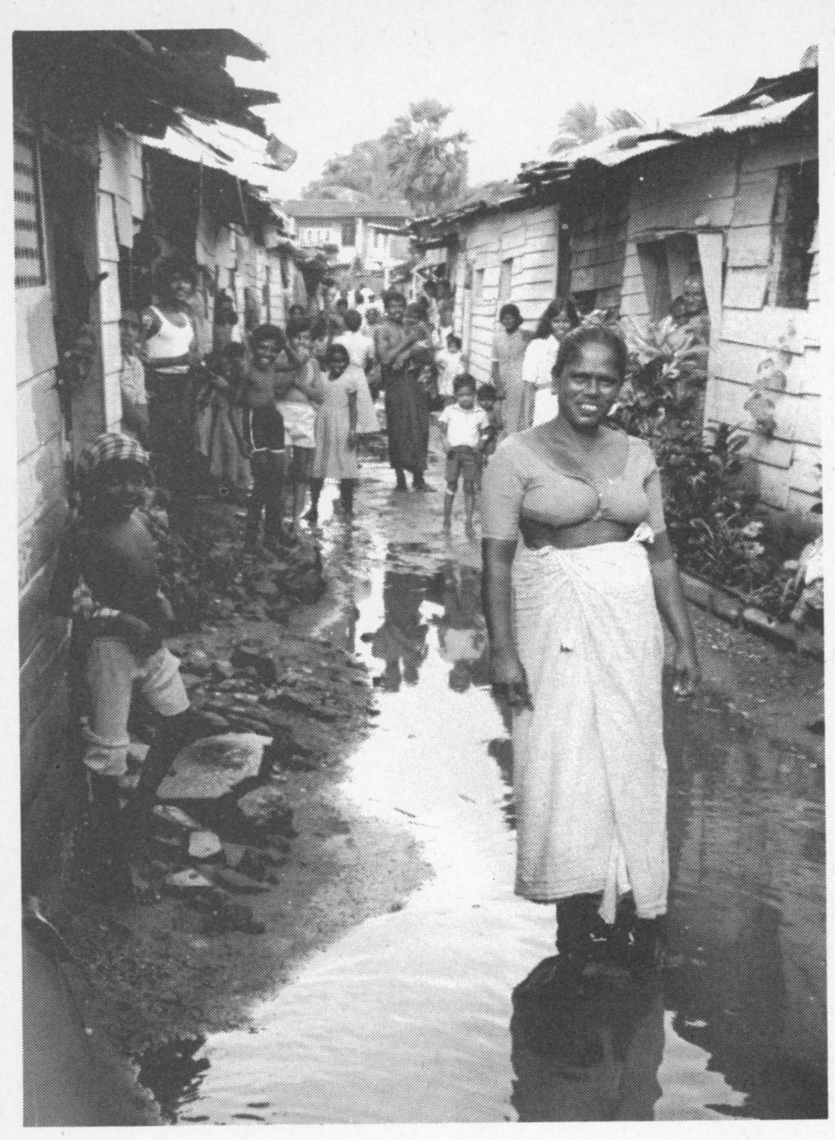

STAGE I - IDENTIFICATION
WHAT ARE THE PROBLEMS?

WHAT ARE THE PROBLEMS?

WHAT IS THE TASK?

The goal is to quickly determine the critical problem areas of a community. The problems are identified by each of the groups involved, according to their expertise and experience, based on observation and interviews.

HOW DO GO ABOUT DOING IT?

A brief field survey will be undertaken by each group. The groups will then list the problems and present them to all of the participants. The problems will be discussed and a master summary list will be prepared.

WHAT IS THE OUTCOME?

Two charts will be prepared: 1) Each group will prepare a chart listing *the problem* they have identified, *why* it is a problem and *to whom* it is a problem. And then, 2) all of the groups will agree on the problems and a master summary chart will be prepared by the Workshop Guide.

HOW DO WE SIT?

Each group is separated at different tables: one community group, one health and social development group, and one technical group.

Your Facilitator should sit with each group and help them in understanding the task and how to go about it. He should briefly orient the group on what his role is, and what he will and will not do.

WHAT MATERIALS AND EQUIPMENT DO WE NEED?

For each group:

- Plan of community
- Checklists to aid survey of community
- Polaroid camera (if available) so you can record and remember the problems
- Tape measure (optional)
- Notebook and pencil for each group member
- Paper for preparing chart
- Tape or pins for displaying chart
- Markers

THINGS TO CONSIDER

- Be sure to clarify the difference between *problems* and *solutions.* In this stage just the *problems* should be identified. How to overcome the problems will be considered next.

- Explain at the beginning why each group is working separately. Make clear that each should identify problems based on their specific expertise.

- Help each group in preparing for the field survey. Suggest things that each group should look out for. Instruct the Facilitator to have in mind specific items about which he can alert his group.

- Encourage everyone from all the groups to see the entire site.

DIRECTIONS FOR ALL GROUPS
(May be copied and used as Handout)

STEP 1 - MAKE A FIELD SURVEY

WHAT IS THE TASK?

You should go into the community and identify what the problems of the community are.

When you identify a problem, see WHY it is a problem, and TO WHOM it is a problem.

Keep note of the problems, so that you can remember them later.

HOW DO YOU GO ABOUT DOING IT?

Organize your group before visiting the community. Maybe prepare a list of "What to Look For".

Divide your group so that they can see the entire site and speak to more families, maybe in teams of three's: "lookers", "askers", and "writers". Be sure you understand *why* it is a problem and to *whom.*

Ask the facilitator to help you to organize your field survey if you need help.

WHAT IS THE OUTCOME?

When you return from the field, each of your team members should have notes which list the problems they have found, and they should know why and to whom they are problems.

DIRECTIONS FOR ALL GROUPS

(May be copied and used as handout)

STEP 2 - LIST THE PROBLEMS

WHAT IS THE TASK?

You should make a LIST of all the things which your group saw as problems.

Explain WHY you think it is a problem, and TO WHOM it is a problem.

WRITE down the problems of your group and the reasons in a chart.

HOW DO YOU GO ABOUT DOING IT?

Select a spokesman from your group and have him prepare the list.

First, list the problems that ALL in your group agree on.

Second, list the problems that SEVERAL people in your group agree on.

Third, list the problems that only a FEW or one person suggests in your group.

Next, find out why some people in your group see some things as problems and others don't. Find out what CRITERIA were used in identifying the problem. Find out HOW they found out it was a problem.

Finally, ONLY LIST the problems that EVERYONE agrees with.

WHAT IS THE OUTCOME?

Your group should fill out a chart indicating the problems, why, and to whom. This list should be a summary of ALL the problems that your group has found, and that your group thinks is important.

Example of CHART to be prepared by each group

PROBLEM	WHY ?	TO WHOM ?
1. [illegible] LAND OWNERSHIP	[illegible] NO DEEDS	[illegible]/261/255 COMMUNITY 261 255
2. [illegible] FLIES	I. [illegible] GARBAGE DUMPING.	[illegible]/261/255 COMMUNITY [illegible]
3. [illegible] DROPOUT (SCHOOLS)	I. [illegible]	[illegible] PRIVATE/CHILDREN
4. [illegible] EMPLOYMENT	I. [illegible]	[illegible] YOUNG PEOPLE
5. [illegible] HOUSING	I. [illegible] POOR II. [illegible] SPACES III. [illegible] LAND OWNERSHIP	[illegible] COM. [illegible] COM:a [illegible] COM.

STEP 3 - AGREE ON PROBLEMS

WHAT IS THE TASK?

All of the groups must AGREE on what the problems are.

The Workshop leader will LIST the problems in which all agree in a summary chart.

HOW DO YOU GO ABOUT DOING IT?

The Workshop Leader will LIST the problems identified by all of the groups into three categories:

Those in which ALL OF THE GROUPS AGREE.

Those in which TWO OF THE GROUPS AGREE.

Those in which NONE OF THE GROUPS AGREE.

Problems in which "all groups agree", and "two groups agree" are automatically added to the agreed list.

Each group can then try to convince the other two groups to add the problem they identified to the list, but which no other group considered a problem.

WHAT IS THE OUTCOME?

At the end of the session all will have agreed on a summary list of the problems. This list represents the problems that all groups feel are the most critical, and in which something should be done.

Example of Summary Chart

SUMMARY LIST – PROBLEMS

WHY? | TO WHOM?

1. HOUSING - නිවාස
2. TOILETS - වැසිකිළි
3. DRINKING WATER - බීමට ජලය
4. FLOODING/DRAINAGE - ජලයෝත් යටවීම කාණු
5. MOSQUITOES - මැසි, මදුරු
6. TENURE - ඉඩම් අයිතිය.
7. ELECTRICITY - විදුලිය.
8. EMPLOYMENT (?) - රැකියා නැතිකම.
9. MALNUTRITION - මන්දපෝෂණය.
10. IMMUNIZATION - එන්නත් කිරීම.

STEP 4 - CONSIDER HEALTH ISSUES

WHAT IS THE TASK?

The community should be made aware of how problems are related to health concerns. The importance of good health should be explained, what they can do about it, and how addressing their problems will directly improve the health situation.

HOW DO GO ABOUT DOING IT?

The Workshop Leader should prepare a matrix listing all of the problems from the summary list of Step 3. Common health concerns of the community should be listed across the top of the list. The Workshop Leader should then call on community representatives to discuss how the problems relate to their health concerns.

WHAT IS THE OUTCOME?

At the end of the session a Summary Chart should be completed which lists the problems of the community as they are related to health issues. The community should be now more aware of how important health is, and how the problems are closely connected with their health. For example, they should understand the importance of personal hygiene, garbage disposal, food preparation and storage, care of drinking water, and sleeping on damp floors.

Example of Summary Chart

PROBLEM	HEALTH CONCERNS: MALNUTRITION	SICKNESS	FOOD PREPARATION	PERSONAL HYGIENE	INFANT WELL-BEING
1. [illegible] LAND OWNERSHIP					
2. මැසි උවදුර FLIES		X	X		X
3. [illegible] DROPOUT (SCHOOLS)					
4. රැකියා නොමැතිකම EMPLOYMENT	X	X			
5. නිවාස. HOUSING		X	X	X	X

STEP 5 - MAKE AND AGREE ON PRIORITIES

WHAT IS THE TASK?

Each team should now determine the ranking of the problems according to their importance. ALL problems should be ranked in order of priority, including health concerns.

HOW DO YOU GO ABOUT DOING IT?

Ask yourself, "which of the problems are really the most important?" Try to make an assessment of each problem in comparison with the rest of the problems.

Each participant should be given a piece of paper to write his own priority list. Workshop leaders should collect the lists and prepare a matrix showing the ranking that each problem has been given by the participants. All problems can then be ordered according to the total marks which each problem gets.

WHAT IS THE OUTCOME?

You willhave a priority list of problems, which includes all of the types of problems identified in the community, including health issues.

Example of priority matrix

	BUILD SPINE ROAD	LOTS/CLUSTER.	SHELTER	WAREHOUSING	FOOD STORAGE	FOOD DISTRIBUTION	COMMUNITY CENTRE	SCHOOLS	WATER DIST.	CLINIC	
SEQUENCE	1	2	3	2	2	2	2	4	2	2	1 = HIGHEST PRIORITY 4 = LEAST
TIME	3	3	2	3	2	3	1	1	2	2	1 = TAKES MOST TIME
COST	2	3	2	1	2	3	1	1	2	1	1 = MOST COSTLY.
INDISP.	1	3	1	2	2	2	3	4	1	2	1 = MOST INDISP.
TOT.	7	11	8	8	8	10	7	10	7	7	LOWEST Nº IS MOST. CRITICAL

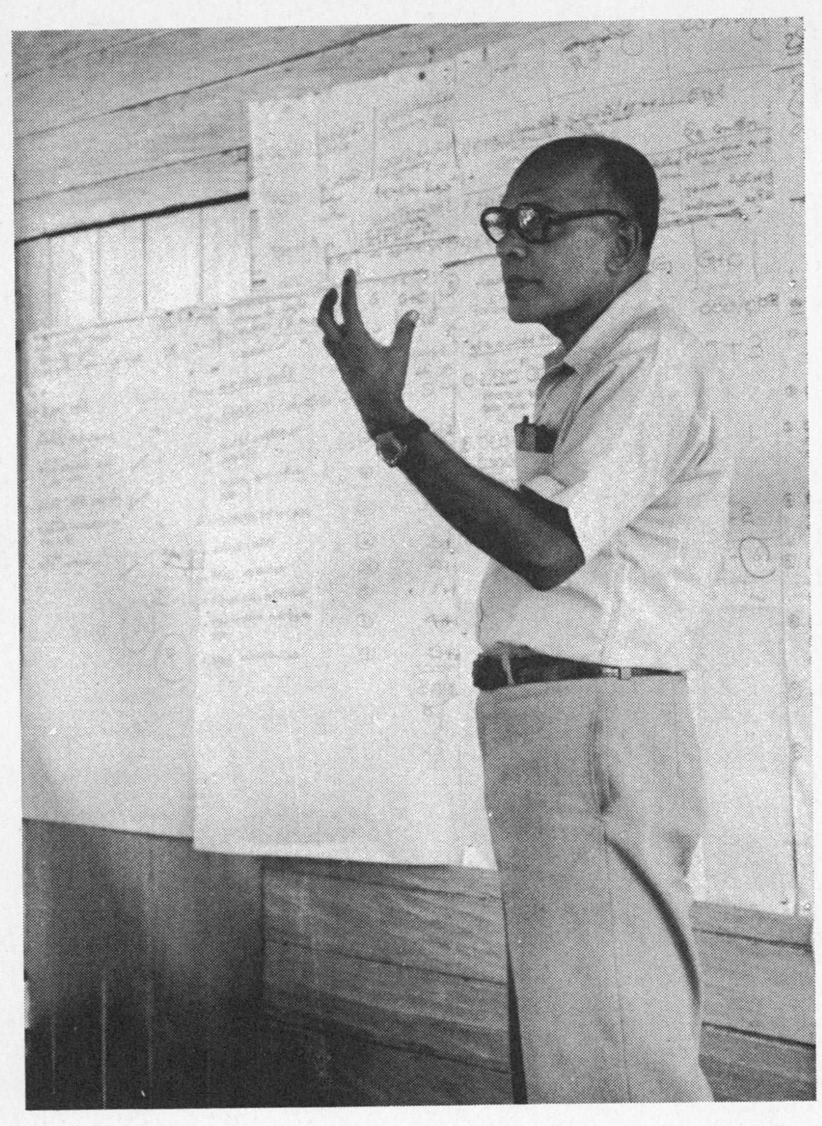

STAGE II - STRATEGIES
WHAT ARE THE APPROACHES?

WHAT ARE THE APPROACHES?

WHAT IS THE TASK?

The goal is to identify in broad terms different ways in dealing with the problems identified in Stage I. Then, agreements must be reached on the priorities of the strategies chosen. You should ask the questions: Which of the ways of tackling the problem serves us best, fits the resources we have, and meets the objectives we have set.

HOW DO YOU GO ABOUT DOING IT?

Each group determines the strategies according to their own point of view. These strategies are prioritized by each group. Through negotiation, a summary list of strategies and their priorities are agreed among the three groups. The workshop leader moderates the sessions, and directs the groups into reaching an agreement. Since there is limited time to these negotiations, there will probably be a number of strategies about which agreement will not have been reached. This is useful in identifying the "sticking points" and extra discussion may be useful on these items.

WHAT IS THE OUTCOME?

Three charts will be prepared:
1) a "List of Strategies" prepared by each group;
2) a listing of "Strategies by Priorities," and
3) a "Summary List of Agreed Strategies."

HOW DO WE SIT?

Each group remains separated during all of the steps. Your Facilitator remains with each group, and helps them to identify strategies and to reach a decision on priorities.

WHAT MATERIALS AND EQUIPMENT DO WE NEED?

For each group:

- Paper for preparing Charts
- Markers
- Tape or pins for displaying charts

THINGS TO CONSIDER

- It is important to properly separate "strategies" from "options" and "tasks".

- All of the groups must agree on the final summary list.

DIRECTIONS FOR ALL GROUPS

(May be copied and used as Handout)

STEP 1 - LIST STRATEGIES

WHAT IS THE TASK?

Your group should take each of the problems agreed on by all of the groups and prepare several general approaches for dealing with them. You should ask yourself: "what kind of approach can we take to do something about the problems?"

HOW DO YOU GO ABOUT DOING IT?

You should divide the broad approaches into IMMEDIATE - things you MUST do now, or LONG-TERM - things that can wait and you can do later. Immediate does not mean "short term"; it does not mean temporary or the time to do it, the effort it will take, or the money needed. The sense of URGENCY is what is important!

WHAT IS THE OUTCOME?

You will have listed a series of broad, general approaches toward solving the problems. Your approaches should be grouped into *immediate* and *long-term.* All of this should be summarized in a chart, and discussed with the other groups.

Example of CHART to be prepared by each group

● PROBLEM	● SHORT TERM	● LONG TERM
	[illegible]	[illegible]
1) [illegible]	[illegible] (1) Repair Existing Hous[es]	[illegible] New housing
2) [illegible] (3)	[illegible] Cleaning Existing Ones	[illegible]
3) [illegible] (2)	[illegible] Provide Extra Ones	[illegible]
4) [illegible] (2)	[illegible] Dig. Cleaning Existing drain	[illegible]
5) [illegible]	[illegible] Clean Environment	[illegible]
6) [illegible] (2)	Legalize [illegible]	[illegible]
7) [illegible]	[illegible] Provision of lamp posts	[illegible]
8) [illegible]	—	[illegible]
9) [illegible] (1)	[illegible] Direct to clinics for treatment	[illegible]
10 [illegible] (3)	[illegible] Immunize	[illegible]
11) [illegible]	[illegible] ?	[illegible]
12 [illegible]	Make ~~proper arrangement~~ to ~~[illegible]~~ to school	[illegible]

DIRECTIONS FOR ALL GROUPS

(May be copied and used as Handout)

STEP 2 - MAKE PRIORITIES

WHAT IS THE TASK?

Each team should now determine which of the broad approaches are the most important. You should rank the approaches:
- those that you feel are the most important (the first priority)
- those that are next in importance (the second priority)
- those that are still important but can wait (the third priority).

You should decide among the members of your team, and place a number on the chart prepared in Step 1.

HOW DO YOU GO ABOUT DOING IT?

Ask yourself, "which of the approaches are really the most important? Which are the ones that need quick, immediate action, and which can be deferred?" You can choose among both the "immediate" and "long-term", since some things that will take a long time may still be very important to the team.

How many first priority things can you select? Everything can be ranked, and you must make that choice. If you were told that only one thing could be done, what would you select? Remember, only chose the things that are *really* important!

WHAT IS THE OUTCOME?

You should have placed 1's by the first priority approaches, 2's by the second priority approaches, and 3's by the third priority approaches.

● PROBLEM [illegible] Housing	Priority	● SHORT TERM [illegible] Repairs	● LONG TERM [illegible]
[illegible]	2	[illegible] Repairs	1. [illegible]
[illegible]	1	1. [illegible] 2. [illegible] water supply [illegible] 3. [illegible] TWIN TAP	1. [illegible]
[illegible]	1	1. [illegible] - Earth filling 2. [illegible] - drains (earth)	1. [illegible]
[illegible]	1	[illegible] spray DDT	1. [illegible] 2. [illegible]
[illegible]	2	1. [illegible] give the [illegible] about Tsunami	1. [illegible] 2. [illegible]
[illegible] ELEC	3	1. [illegible] Temporary Supply	1. [illegible]
[illegible]	2	1. [illegible] 1. [illegible] 2. [illegible] 3. [illegible] direct to the Govt institutes	1. [illegible]
[illegible]	1	1. [illegible] 2. [illegible] Provide Thriposha & Kola Kanda	1. [illegible]
[illegible]		1. [illegible] direct to the clinic	1. [illegible]
[illegible]		1. —	1. [illegible] 2. [illegible]
[illegible] DROPOUTS	3	1. [illegible] Direct to schools	1. [illegible]
[illegible]		1. [illegible] Under the tree	1. [illegible]

DIRECTIONS FOR ALL GROUPS

(May be copied and used as Handout)

STEP 3 - AGREE ON PRIORITIES

WHAT IS THE TASK?

You must now agree with the other groups on what are the few most important approaches that must be taken first. Keep in mind that all are problems, but which ones would be tackled first?

HOW DO WE GO ABOUT DOING IT?

One way to help in deciding is to make a box with three rows: in the first list all of the approaches which are considered the most important by all of the groups, in the second list all of the approaches considered second in importance, and in the third, the last in importance. This way you will see which ones have been chosen by each of the groups very quickly. Even now as you list the approaches, you may already eliminate some now that you have thought and discussed them further.

Once you have the chart prepared, each team should select a few of their choices which were not considered for the first priority but which they feel strongly should be included. Also, if a team feels that the first choices of some other team shouldn't be there, they should bring it up for the groups' attention and consideration. If there is no discussion, all of the first choices will be the selected actions, and all of the seconds and thirds will be eliminated.

WHAT IS THE OUTCOME?

You should have prepared a SUMMARY OF THE AGREED FIRST CHOICES for the community. These will be the ones that will be further developed in the next stages.

Example of CHART to be prepared by each team

	ALL AGREE සියලු දෙනා එකඟයි	2 AGREE කණ්ඩායම් 2 ක් එකඟයි	1 CHOSEN කණ්ඩායම් 1 ක් එකඟයි
PRIORITY ① මූලික ප්‍රමුඛතාවය.		HOUSE REPAIR CLEAN/REPAIR EXISTING TOILETS. MALNUTRITION	USE TEMP. LOCATION FOR COMMUNITY CENTRE ~~MALNUTRITION~~ INCREASE WATER PRESSURE EARTH FILL LOW LAND & MAKE DRAINS TO RD. ~~SPRAY DDT~~ BOIL/COOL WATER (Ed...) MORE SELF EMPLOYMENT
PRIORITY ② ද්විතීය ප්‍රමුඛතාවය		PROVIDE SECURITY OF TENURE	PROVIDE MORE WATER POINTS. REPAIR TOILETS MAKE MORE JOBS CLEAN DRAINS REMOVE GARBAGE ENCOURAGE ATTENDANCE TO CLINICS ED. FOR FAMILY PLANNING
PRIORITY ③ තෘතීය ප්‍රමුඛතාවය.		USE EXISTING BUILDING / + HELP OF NGO FOR PRE SCHOOL.	~~USE EXISTING BUILDING FOR PRE SCHOOL~~ IMMUNISATION HOUSE REPAIRS CONNECT TEMP. TO ELECT. SUPPLY FAMILY PLANNING (FOR OVERCROWDING) EDUCATE PARENTS RE DROPOUTS

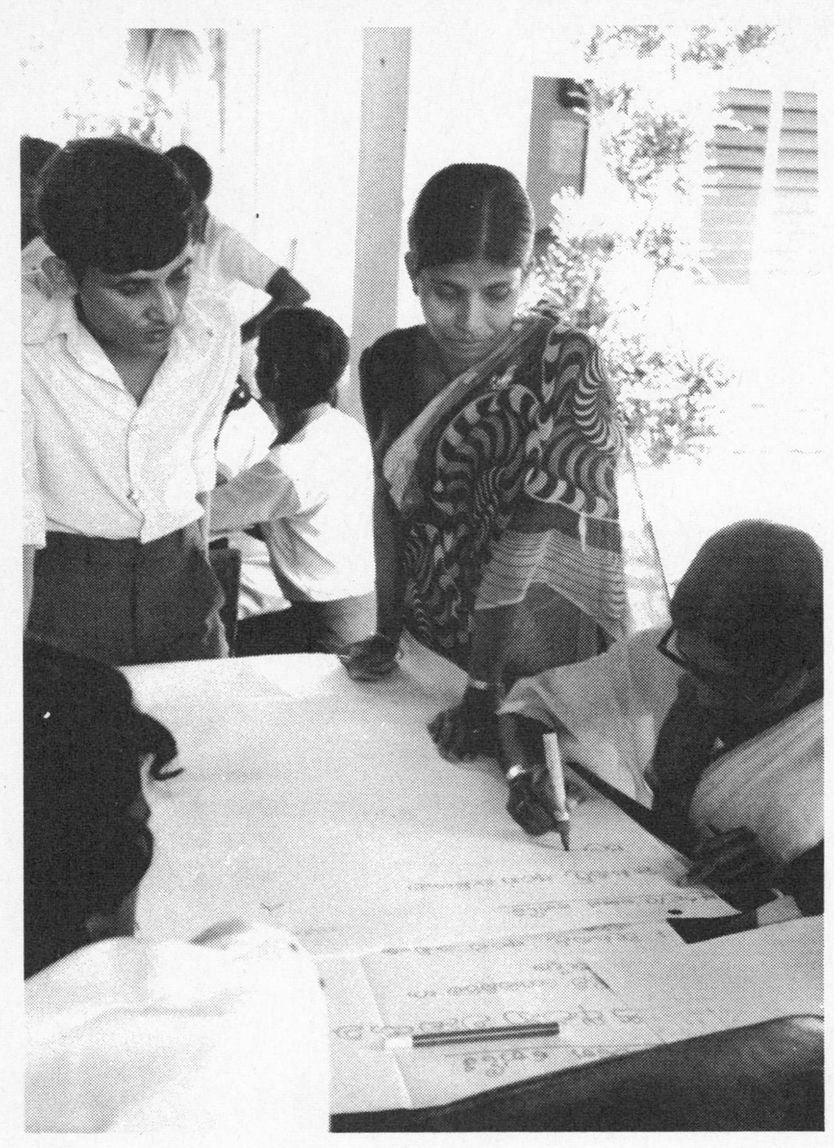

STAGE III – OPTIONS AND TRADEOFFS
WHAT ARE THE ACTIONS?

WHAT ARE THE ACTIONS?

WHAT IS THE TASK?

The goal is to identify several ways of carrying out the broad strategies agreed upon in Stage II. Then, we must select from these alternative solutions the few that are the most important to all three groups.

HOW DO WE GO ABOUT DOING IT?

The technical group and social and health group will identify a range of options for solving the problems following the agreed general strategies. They then will determine the costs to the government and to the community for each option. In the next step, the community group will join the other group and the three will negotiate and agree on the most important option. Selection will be in a situation of "much money," and one when there is "little money." Representatives of each team will prepare a final summary chart of the agreed options.

WHAT IS THE OUTCOME?

Three charts will be prepared:
1) The first chart lists the available options in solving the priority problems. Along with each option, the cost to both the government and the community will be identified.
2) The second chart lists all of the selected options, when there is "much money."
3) The third chart lists the priority options when there is "little money."

HOW DO WE SIT?

During the first step, the community group will not be present.

The technical group and the health and social development groups will be divided into two mixed teams: each team will have one-half of the technical group with one-half of the health and social development group. During the second step, the community group will be divided between the two teams.

WHAT MATERIALS AND EQUIPMENT DO WE NEED?

For each group:

- Paper for preparing chart
- Markers
- Tape or pins for displaying charts

THINGS TO CONSIDER

- The technical group and the health and social development groups have the responsibility to prepare reasonable *relative* costs for each of the options. Two sets of costs are prepared; in one, the government will assume full responsibility; in the other, the government is helped with contributions from the community. Keep in mind that in some cases the community will not be able to contribute at all. In other cases the community will be able to do everything by itself.

- Make sure that the options are clear enough and *different* enough so everyone understands them.

- The choice of options is essentially the responsibility of the community representatives. The technical group is only to explain the options and to make clear the implications.

- From past experience, some of the workshops adopted a different way to choose among the options, which eliminated the relative costs as presented in Step 2. The terms merely let each team decide among themselves which are priorities and what would be the contribution of the community. Then, a chart similar to Step 3 in Stage II "Agree on Priorities" was used to make the final list.

DIRECTIONS FOR ALL GROUPS

(May be copied and used as Handout)

STEP 1 - LIST OPTIONS

WHAT IS THE TASK?

You should do two things: First - You should take *each* broad strategy and develop several ways of satisfying the problem. Second - you should estimate the relative cost for doing the work. You should consider this cost in three ways, 1) the government does all of the work and pays all of the costs; 2) the community and government share in the work and the costs; and, 3) the community does all of the work and pays all the costs.

HOW DO WE GO ABOUT DOING IT?

You should divide up the strategies so all of them are considered. Then you should develop several different ways of carrying out the strategy. You may want to start at the simplist way of doing it - which is often the cheapest - and then continue until you develop the most involved way of doing it - which is usually the most expensive. For example, if the community needed a place to meet to discuss community concerns, the simplist way of doing it is to designate a place under a tree, and the only thing you would need are some chairs and perhaps a sign. Another alternative is to ask the government to build a community center, which will be expensive and take a while before it can be built. But then, if you ask the government to do this, they may not have money left over to do other things you may need more. So, another way to do it is for the community to contribute by clearing the land and helping in the construction, this would be quicker and lower the costs, and leave money for other community needs.

Once you have decided on different ways to do things, you should determine the relative costs. Because we do not know the real costs right now, we just need to see how they relate to each other. The Technical Group members can help in determining this. Let us agree that the most expensive thing to be done will have a cost of

"9", and that everything has a cost, there is no "0" or free thing to be had. The community can also contribute their efforts in terms of work and money, and this should also be calculated. So, for each of the options, first estimate how much it would cost if the government had to pay for it all, and then see what he community could contribute and estimate how much less the government would have to pay then.

WHAT IS THE OUTCOME?

You should have completed a list of different options for each of the broad strategies. Your team may have only prepared the options for a few of the strategies, since everyone will be doing different ones. Then, for each of the options, you should have determined the cost if the government did all of the work and pay all of the costs, and second, if the community shared in the work and the costs.

Example of CHART to be prepared by each team

• Community Centre.

Option	G.	G+C
1. Tent – Permanent.	–	0+3 (3)
2. Temporary Shed	(4)	(2)+2 (4)
3. under a tree. (255)	–	0+1 (1)
4 Permanent Building	9	(4)+2 (6)
5.	1	0+1 (1)

DIRECTIONS FOR ALL GROUPS

(May be copied and used as Handout)

STEP 2 - NEGOTIATE AND SELECT OPTIONS

WHAT IS THE TASK?

You should now reach a decision as to which options are the most important and able to be afforded. You must reach a decision at two levels: If the government had lots of funds to help, which of the options would you select? And secondly, (and realistically!) which are the really critical options that the groups feel is the minimum necessary.

HOW DO WE GO ABOUT DOING IT?

You have to balance the amount of money available, and the contributions of the community. The more the community contributes, the further the money and support from the government will go. The amount of the government's contribution will remain the same, but the efforts of the community can change: if the community agrees to work additional days (or even evenings...) then more can be accomplished.

Keep in mind that it is not just the funds of the government that limit what can be selected, but also the contributions of the community in terms of work and money. Be realistic: don't promise too much from the community! You all have other responsibilities and must attend to them first.

WHAT IS THE OUTCOME?

You should come out with a summary list of the selected options, along with the contributions of the government and the contributions of the community. You should find the total of both contributions.

Example of CHART to be prepared by each team

	(G)	(G+C)
රූ: 40 යමනේ බෝර්ඩ්.		
① නිවාස අළුත් වැඩියාව නිවාස 30 ක් අළුතින් තැනීම සහ ඉතිරිය වෙනත් ප්‍රජාතයකට ගොයම.		5 + 3
② ප්‍රජාශාලාව - ස්ථිර ගොඩනැගිල්ලක්		4 + 2
③ ජලය සැපයීම හා වැව් දියුණු කිරීම. ජල කරාම වැඩි කිරීම. ජල හල ළිඳකට වෙනස්කිරීම.		4 + 1 1 + 1
④ මන්දපෝෂණය පෝෂ්‍ය ආහාර ලබාදීම මව්වරුන්ට උපදෙස්දීම.	3 2	
⑤ ආදායම් මාර්ග වැඩිකිරීම කාර්මික පාඨමාලා. ණය ලබාදීම	3 4	
⑥ පහත් ප්‍රදේශ ගොඩකිරීම කානු සැපයීම රජය මගින් ද්‍රව්‍ය ලබාදීම		4 + 2
⑦ පවුල් සංවිධානය අවබෝධය ලබාදීම	5	
⑧ වැසිකිළි අළුත්වැඩියාව උපකරණ හා ද්‍රව්‍ය සැපයීම		3 + 2
	17	21 + 11 = **38**

Glaxo

STAGE IV - PLANNING FOR IMPLEMENTATION
WHO DOES WHAT WHEN AND HOW?

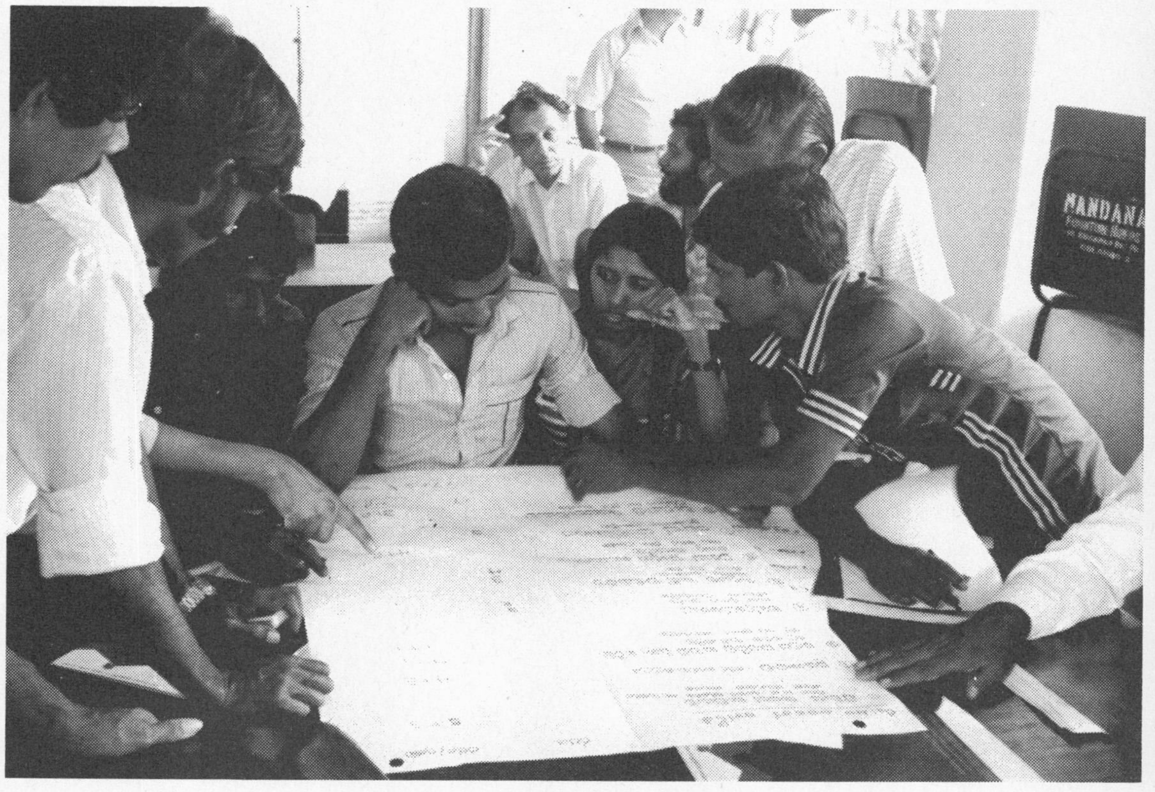

WHO DOES WHAT WHEN AND HOW?

WHAT IS THE TASK?

The goal is to prepare a step-by-step plan of action in implementing the priority options. The action plans should address the question of WHO, WHAT, and HOW, and define in more detail the physical planning requirement for the site and selected dwellings.

HOW DO GO ABOUT DOING IT?

Each team will prepare a chart of the necessary tasks. They will present to invited officials who will comment on the feasibility of the program.

WHAT IS THE OUTCOME?

The product is a plan of action for the upgrading components. Two types of charts will be prepared:
1) A "Task Chart" which lists in detail the step-by-step tasks in implementing each priority option; and
2) Plans which explain in more detail the specific improvements to the site and to selected dwellings.

HOW DO WE SIT?

Each of the teams will be divided so all of the priority options will be addressed. Make sure that there are representatives from each of the groups on each team.

WHAT MATERIALS AND EQUIPMENT DO WE NEED?

For each team:

- Paper for charts
- Markers
- Tape or pins for attaching charts to wall

THINGS TO CONSIDER

- The invited observers should be drawn from the various agencies who will be involved in the upgrading. If no one else is available, select observers from among the participants who have exhibited technical competence.

- The technical group members should take the lead in the preparation of the tasks. The community group members should indicate how the community can best contribute.

- Step 2 (Alternative B) "Identify Needed House Improvements" may already be carried out under another program. For example, the "Housing Information Service" covers these aspects. Therefore, only if no other workshop is planned on housing need this step be included.

DIRECTIONS FOR ALL GROUPS

(May be copied and used as Handout)

STEP 1 - LIST TASKS

WHAT IS THE TASK?

For each of the Options agreed upon as being a priority, a detailed, step-by-step work program should be identified. On a chart, you should list the TASKS of the work program, and with each task identify the following:

- WHAT are the tasks? What needs to be done step-by-step in carrying out the work? What needs to be done first, what next, and what last? You should include "maintenance" as the last task in all of the work programs.
- WHO will do the task? Should it be done by the NHDA, a community member, or someone else? If the community is to do the work, have they agreed that they would actually do it, and do they have the time?
- WHAT and HOW is the task to be done? What kind of tools will be needed? When will the work be carried out, on the weekends? in the evenings?

HOW DO WE GO ABOUT DOING IT?

Divide the teams so all options are considered. You should have the member from the technical group take the lead in outling the tasks, and help him with suggestions on how the community could help.

WHAT IS THE OUTCOME?

You should have a chart filled out which lists the options and all of the steps necessary to carry it out. (If you find that the costs are too high, then you should go back to Stage III: Step 2: Negotiate and select options.)

Example of CHART to be prepared for each OPTION by the teams

BUILD COMMUNITY CENTRE

• WHAT [illegible]	• WHO. [illegible]	• HOW. [illegible]
IDENTIFY SITE	COMMUNITY :	SURVEY.
	OTHERS : NHDA. U.C.	BUY LAND. PREPARE (FILL)
MAKE A PLAN.	C	
	O NHDA	USING STANDARDS LOOKING SOME EXAMPLES CHECKING HOW ITS BEING USED
APPROVE PLAN.	C	
	O	
PREPARE FOR CONSTRUCTION	C	
	O	
BUILD.	C	
	O	
~	C	
	O	

(Alternate A)

STEP 2 - LOCATE PLANNED SITE IMPROVEMENTS

WHAT IS THE TASK?

You should identify the locations of the agreed options on a plan of the community. Keep in mind that location is one of the most critical decisions in many of the things provided in a community; for example, the placement of a standpipe. First, there are the technical questions (for example, the easy, economical connection to a water main) and then there are the social issues, for location can impose hardships on families if not carefully considered. For example, carrying water can be made difficult for everybody if standpipes are not properly located.

You may want to divide the work and have different teams locate different things.

Locating the things that the community wants to do on a plan will help the community to coordinate the placement and implementation of the elements, so that no difficulties occur when being built. Also, it will help in deciding on the number of things to provide, for example, streetlights.

HOW DO WE GO ABOUT DOING IT?

First, review the agreed options and identify those items that require deciding on a location. Then, sketch in the tentative location, after discussion with the members in your group. It may be useful to go back to the community and actually decide on the location by placing a marker on the spot. This way, everyone can better understand where things are to be built.

When you are locating the things, keep in mind that the walking distance should be kept as small as possible so that everyone can use the facility. Also, particularly when locating a standpipe which lots of people will use and which will create standing water and mud, are the neighboring families aware of the inconvenience?

WHAT IS THE OUTCOME?

At the end of the session you should have a sketch plan of the community on which the physical options are located. It would be useful to include a brief description of the reasons for locating the option.

Example of Sketch of Planned Site Improvements

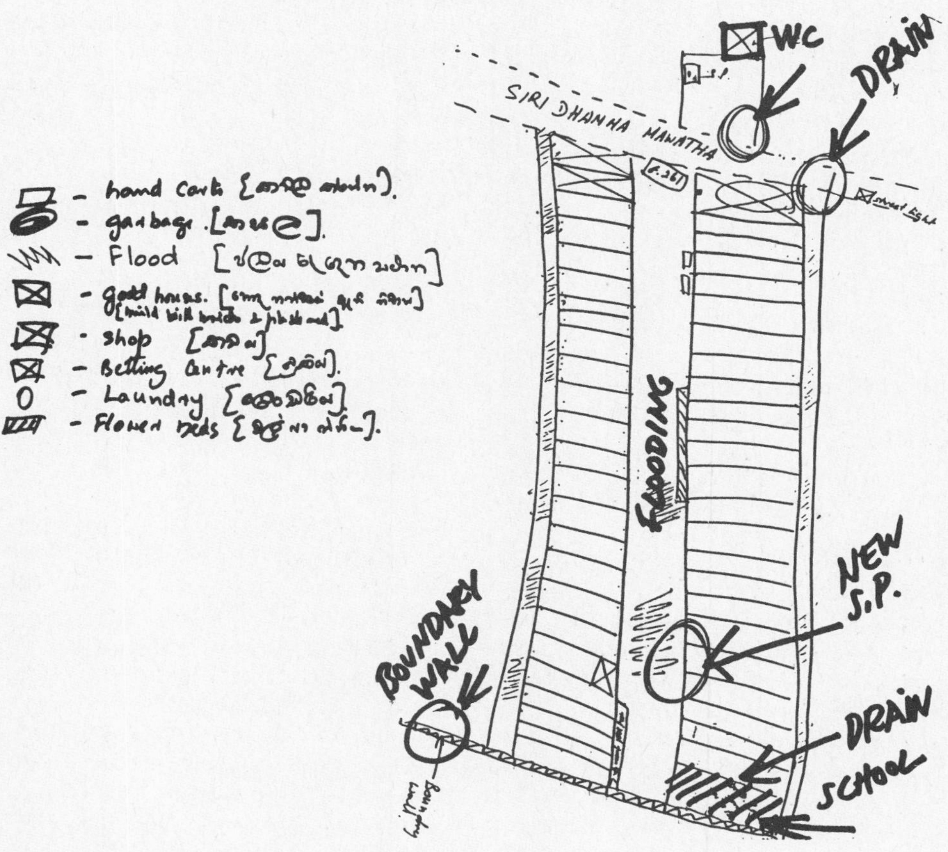

(Alternate B)

STEP 2 - IDENTIFY NEEDED HOUSE IMPROVEMENTS

WHAT IS THE TASK?

You should identify the problems of the houses in the community. You should look at the construction, particularly from the health and safety standpoint, and make a judgment about what improvements can be made. Look for things that may affect a family's health, for example, poor ventilation, and smoke in the rooms from cooking, or perhaps damp, cold floors on which the family sleeps.

First, *sketch a plan* of the house, and indicate the problem areas.

Next, make a *list of observations* of thing that are bad.

Then, you should think of suggestions or *recommendations* which you could make on how to improve the situation.

HOW DO WE GO ABOUT DOING IT?

You should divide into teams, with each responsible for looking at several houses. Before you start, discuss among yourselves some of the problem areas to look for. It may be useful to prepare a checklist of points to guide the team, but do not limit yourself to only the checklist!

Next, go back to the community and find the houses you are assigned to. Your team should measure the house (use your feet as a yardstick!) and draw a sketch which indicates the main elements (rooms, cooking area, windows, etc.). Make a list of the things you observed to be bad and take notes so they can be combined later on in a summary sheet.

After you return to the meeting room, prepare a summary of the things you did: sketch the house plan and section showing the main features; make a summary list of the observations from your team members; and now think of recommendations you could make to improve the house. Keep in mind that some things are more important than others and should be strongly suggested to be done quickly. Also, don't forget that some things will cost more money or will take a long time to do anything about it.

WHAT IS THE OUTCOME?

Each team should have sketched several plans of houses along with observations on the problems and suggestions on how to make improvements. These should be presented to the community, for many of the problems will apply to other houses as well. This information should help the families in deciding how to improve their houses. They now will know where they need help. If some of the problems occur throughout the community, the technical staff could arrange future meetings and discuss in detail what and how improvements could be made.

Example of Sketch of Needed House Improvements

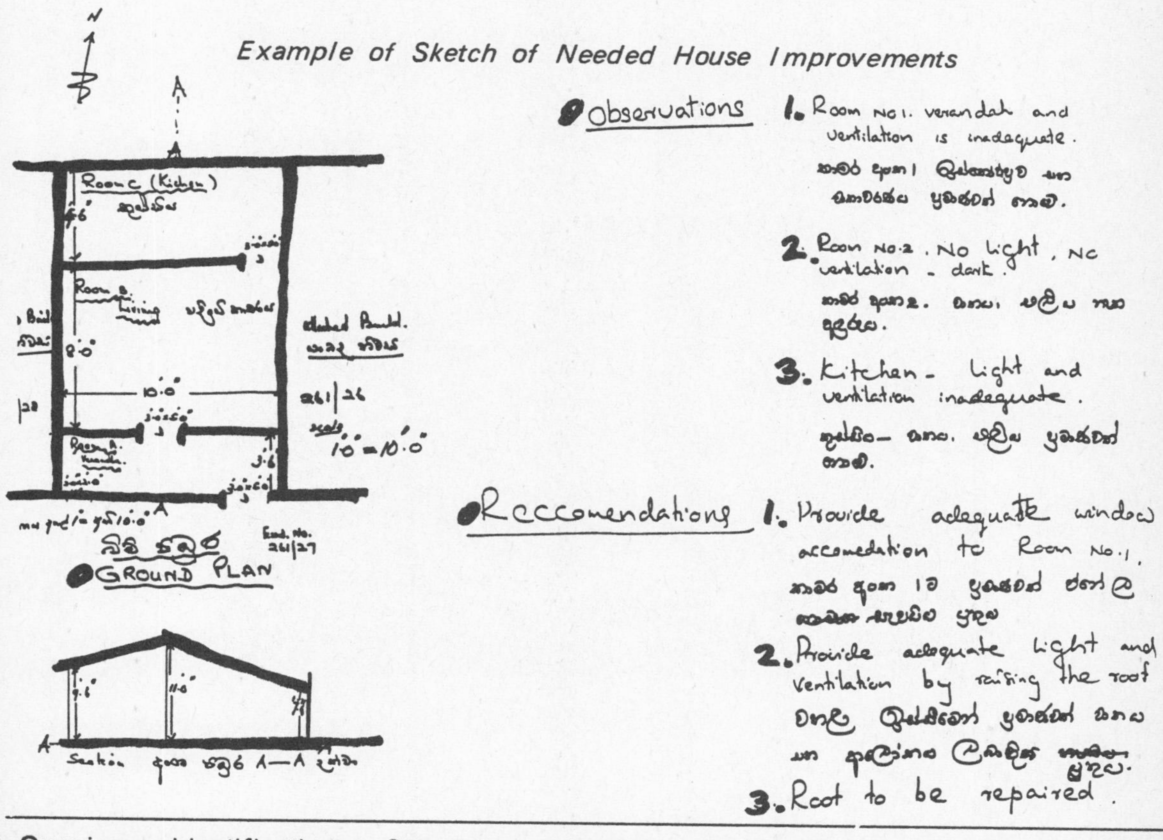

N
A
Room C (Kitchen)
Room B. Living
10'0"
10'0" = 10'0"
GROUND PLAN
Section
Observations
1. Room No 1. verandah and ventilation is inadequate.
2. Room No.2. No light, No ventilation - dark.
3. Kitchen - light and ventilation inadequate.
Reccomendations
1. Provide adequate window accomedation to Room No. 1.
2. Provide adequate light and ventilation by raising the roof
3. Roof to be repaired.

STAGE V – MONITORING
HOW IS IT WORKING?
AND WHAT CAN WE LEARN?

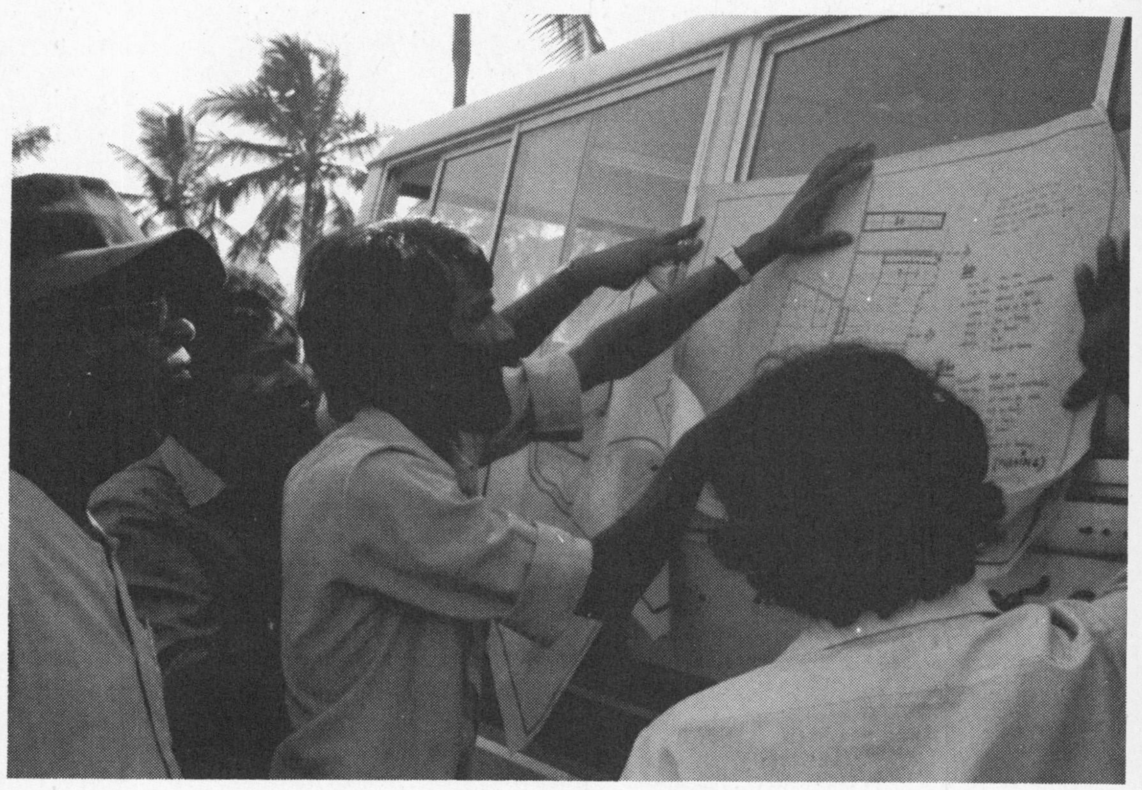

HOW IS IT WORKING? AND WHAT CAN WE LEARN?

WHAT IS THE TASK?

The primary goal is to learn from previous efforts, and to incorporate the experience into the next improvements for the community. This experience is a check on "how things worked", both in implementation and in programming.

This stage can only carried out in communities after improvements have been made. It may be useful to do this stage first, and use this stage to identify the problems, both old and new, and then proceed with the other stages I, II, III, and IV.

HOW DO WE GO ABOUT DOING IT?

The community and the project officer will identify the things planned for improvement previously. Then, the teams will review what the situation is and what can be learned.

HOW DO WE SIT?

The efforts are jointly carried out by all of the participants. For convenience when there are many things to look at, teams could be formed, with each reviewing the situation in detail.

WHAT IS THE OUTCOME?

Each group should have two charts filled out, one which summarizes the situation of the improvements made peviously, and the other, what was learned. Maintenance issues are also looked at, and included in the charts.

WHAT MATERIALS AND EQUIPMENT DO WE NEED?

For each team:

- Paper for preparing charts
- Markers
- Tape or pins for displaying charts
- Notebook for taking notes in community interviews and observations

THINGS TO CONSIDER

- It is important to go back into the community and look at the improvements. It is not sufficient to just ask the community representatives at the meeting. Be sure to talk to other families also.

DIRECTIONS FOR ALL GROUPS

(May be copied and used as handout)

STEP 1 - DESCRIBE THE SITUATION

WHAT IS THE TASK?

You should first list all of the improvements planned in a previous workshop. For each of these items, you should describe the situation, both positively and negatively. Ask the question: "What has been done? How does it work? If something is not working well, what is the problem?" For example, a new standpipe may be well located, but the water supply may be inadequate.

You should also include a review on how maintenance is being handled. Find out who is responsible for maintenance, and how it is succeeding.

HOW DO WE GO ABOUT DOING IT?

It may be useful to divide up into teams. The teams should include respresentatives from the community as well as from the technical and health groups; do not just have technical staff look at technical items! The best approach is to have each team look at all of the improvements. However, in some circumstances it may be better to divide up and have each team look at different things. For example, one team could be responsible for all infrastructure matters, one for all community facilities that were built.

The teams should go into the community and directly observe the situation, and talk to other families about their opinion. Maybe they have good suggestions for next time or how to improve things in other communities.

WHAT IS THE OUTCOME?

A chart should be prepared that lists the improvements, how they are working and what are the problems and successes. For each item, there should be a review if adequate maintenance is being undertaken.

Example of Summary Chart

• WHAT WAS IMPROVED? [illegible]	• HOW IS IT WORKING? [illegible]	• WHO MAINTAINS IT? [illegible]
1. WATER SUPPLY WITH NEW WELLS. [illegible]		
2. SOME PATHS/ ROADS. [illegible]		
3. SITE DRAINAGE ALONGSIDE NEW PATHS. [illegible]		
4. NEW LATRINES [illegible]		
5. HEALTH EDUCATION - POSTERS. - TRAIN VOLUNTEERS - MALNUTRIT. [illegible]		

DIRECTIONS FOR ALL GROUPS
(May be copied and used as handout)

STEP 2 - DRAW LESSONS FROM EXPERIENCE

WHAT IS THE TASK?

Each team should review the positive and negative experiences and the maintenance issues identified in Step 1. For each item, you should now try to answer two questions: What can be learned in general for future micro-planning? and, What can be done to correct or improve things in the community?

HOW DO WE GO ABOUT DOING IT?

The same teams from the previous step should not fill out a chart which summarizes the recommendations and suggestions for improvement. The chart has three columns: the *first* again lists the planned improvements, the *second* lists recommendations in general, and the *third* lists the specific suggestions for your community.

WHAT IS THE OUTCOME?

A chart should be prepared which points out the lessons for next time. Two types of lessons should be identified: ones that can act as general guidelines and ones that make specific recommendations for your community. These lessons can be used to initiate another Micro-Planning workshop, and can be used immediately by the Project Officer and the community to improve the present situation.

Example of Summary Chart

STATUS IMPROVEMENT MADE	WHAT SHOULD BE DONE **TO CORRECT** THINGS FOR THIS SITE.	WHAT SHOULD BE DONE **TO AVOID** SAME MISTAKES NEXT TIME.
1. DRAINS POORLY LAID TO FALLS CAUSING FLOODING ELSEWHERE ON SITE & ARE FRANKLY A HEALTH HAZARD.		
2.		
3.		
4.		
5.		

THE CLOSING SESSION

THE CLOSING SESSION

WHAT IS THE TASK?

The goal of this session is to review all workshop activities and to have each groups summarize its understanding of the activities and what it agrees should be the next steps in the improvement of the community. The outcome should be presented to the remainder of the community.

Before the closing session, the wall charts of the workshops should be quickly reviewed so that any particular problems that might have been omitted could be discussed. When it is time to present the outcome of the workshop to the whole community, all of the workshop participants should be conversant with the various aspects of the work plan.

The goal of the closing session is to review and summarize the workshop material and reach agreement on what the next steps in the improvement of the community should be. In addition, where re-location of a certain number of families is involved in the improvement programme, this issue will need to be brought to the attention of the full community. However, it should be pointed out that no decision as to who should leave and who should remain in the site was taken during the workshop. This decision has to be taken by the whole community in consultation with each other on the basis of a community consensus.

HOW TO GO ABOUT DOING IT?

The workshop leader will call on a representative from each of the three groups to review the activities and present them to the remainder of the community:

The Community Representative: he should comment on how the choices reflect the priority concerns of the community and review how the community has agreed to contribute in solving the problems.

The NHDA Representative: he should review the feasibility of the options and clarify the next steps. Most importantly, he should set a timetable for when the choices will be implemented, and who the "contact person" is at the NHDA (and how to get in touch with him).

The Health Official: he should review how the selected options address the health concerns of the community and those of the health officials. He should summarize the next steps from his agency and the timetable for implementation. It may be useful to also identify a person to contact if there are questions.

After all have spoken, the workshop leader should review what were the objectives and what has been achieved, and thank the community for hosting the workshop. It may be good to "formally" sign a "contract" agreement by all parties: the community, the NHDA, and the health officials. This would be a symbolic document that could be posted in the community meeting place as a remainder of the tasks and agreements. Three copies should be signed, one for each of the parties. Placing the document in a glass frame would protect it and and allow it to be hung in an open space.

WHAT IS THE OUTCOME?

It is important that the following should be agreed: a **TIMETABLE** for implementation, a **CONTACT PERSON** in the NHDA, and the **NEXT MEETING DATE** with the whole community.

HOW DO WE SIT?

All the groups will be together. Participants are encouraged to sit with other groups and not stay with their group. The WHOLE COMMUNITY should be invited, as well as other officials from the NHDA and the health agencies.

WHAT MATERIALS AND EQUIPMENT DO WE NEED?

All of the charts should be pinned or taped to the walls. They should be arranged in sequence to facilitate explanation to the community. The summary program should be at the center so the various speakers may quickly refer to it.

Three copies of a final agreement document, each framed with glass, should be provided for the last session.

THINGS TO CONSIDER

- Make sure that there are enough benches or seats for the whole community.
- Try to keep the session very short, since everyone is probably tired and probably many have to stand.
- It is important to hold the summary session the same day as the workshop ends. Do not postpone it, as people will forget what happened or the momentum will be lost.
- Try to get higher officials from all the agencies to attend. This will give a boost in credibility to the commitments.
- It may be desirable to let the community leader end the session, since he has been the host for the workshop.

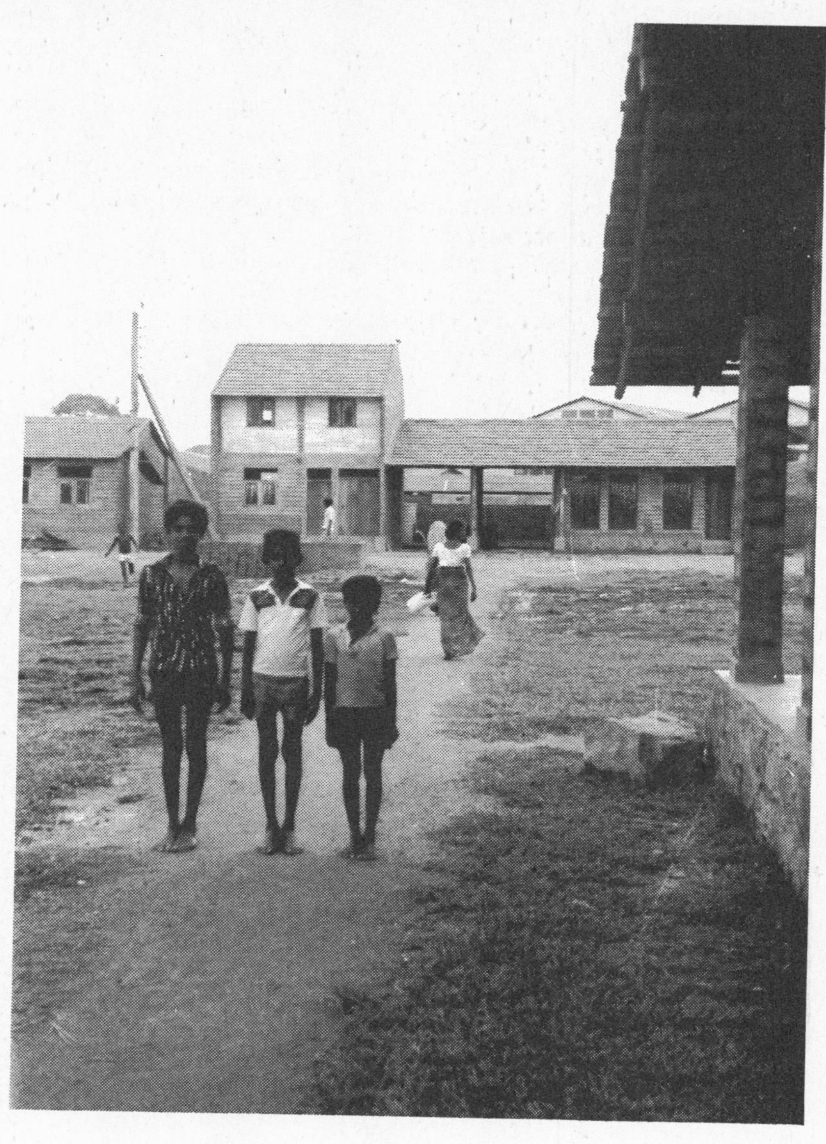

AFTER THE WORKSHOP - DOCUMENTATION

WHAT IS THE TASK?

The goals is to make the whole community aware of the outcome of the workshop.

HOW DO WE GO ABOUT DOING IT?

Select the sections of the workshop outcomes which are important to the community. These may include the priority list of problems in Stage I, Step 5, and the implementation plan of Stage IV, Step 1.

Then, reproduce a sufficient number of copies for distribution among all of the members of the community, government officials involved in the implementation, and others involved in the process; for example, health officials.

WHAT MATERIALS AND EQUIPMENT DO WE NEED?

- Equipment to make copies quickly and economically
(This may include stencils and the necessary machines to copy them.)

OUTCOME

A printed document which consists of important sections of the workshop.

AFTER THE WORKSHOP - FOLLOW-UP

WHAT IS THE TASK?

The primary effort should be directed to see that the agreements are being carried out by all of the groups. All groups should follow-up the work and not let it fall behind or get pushed off till later. This includes the community members, as well as the housing officials, and the UNICEF officials.

HOW DO WE GO ABOUT DOING IT?

The primary responsibility for day-to-day supervision is the Local Project Officer from the government side, and the community leaders from the community. The Workshop Leader does not have direct responsibility anymore, and the the Logistics Officer from the Central Office is in the best position to check periodically that things are moving.

THE KEY TO SUCCESS IS WHEN THINGS DO NOT GET DELAYED!

The community should see that there are positive results for their efforts. This will encourage them to willingly contribute their labor in carrying out their agreed tasks.

The Workshop Leader should reflect on the workshop and make a self-assessment: Did the community understand what he was explaining? Was the outcome positive? What improvements should be made next time? How could the Workshop be restructured next time to make it more successful?